Image to Image
Volume II

by

Rita Kugler Carmack

JEWEL PRESS
Box   904
Fort Collins, Colorado 80522

Image to Image -- Volume II
ISBN 0-937093-00-9
Copyright © 1986 by Rita Kugler Carmack
JEWEL PRESS® Pulisher
P. O. Box 904
Ft. Collins, CO 80522

Dedication

It is with joy that I dedicate this book to my husband, Derin.

I thank God for the love we share and for the spiritual support Derin is to me as I write books and minister to people.

Acknowledgements

I thank the Lord for His help in the writing of this book.

I would like to thank my daughter, Starlyn, for her editorial help, my secretary, Anna, for typing and proofreading the manuscript, and my nephew, Brian, for putting it on the computer system.

I also appreciate the many hours spent by Sheila Cogan, taking photographs of the beautiful flowers in my yard, one of which is the cover photo.

Contents

Foreword

This is *Volume Two* in what will be a four volume series that will provide devotional readings for one full year when finished.

If you do not have *Volume I* of *Image to Image*, I suggest you read it first as it contains foundational teachings that will enhance your understanding of *Volume II*.

My goal for writing this series of devotional books is to help Christians mature and become victorious in their everyday lives.

In this book, as in *Volume I* of this devotional series, I encourage you to be a *"doer"* of the Word and not merely an unfruitful hearer who doesn't apply God's truth in your life.

The suggested affirmations and related scriptures are to be spoken aloud everyday until you have victory in a specific area of your life. In overcoming some habits and temptations, you will need to apply God's truth for a long period of time, while just a few days may take care of other situations.

I hope you will make a quality decision to make God's Word a part of your very heart and spirit so that it becomes "automatic" to quote whenever satan tempts you to sin or to doubt God's promises.

Through His Word, God causes us to be *"more than conquerors."* As you read the scriptures presented, please pray that your spiritual eyes will be opened and that the truth of the Bible will become alive and active in your heart.

Here is my prayer for you:

"Dear Lord, as my friends use this book, I pray that their hearts will be open to the truth of Your Word.

"Help them to make a strong commitment to daily use Your Word to strengthen their spirits, renew their minds and deepen their walk with You.

"Lord, as Christians we want to have correct attitudes and fruitful lives so that others will see the light of Jesus in us and be drawn to Him.

"In the precious Name of Jesus I pray, Amen."

God loves you - and so do I!

Rita Carmack
February 1986

Week 14
Walking in Divine Health

Week 14 Day 1
God's Word Brings Life

The Lord will keep you free from every disease...
Deuteronomy 7:15

Deuteronomy 5 contains the 10 commandments of
God. Chapters 6 & 7 tell the children of Israel to love and
obey God and give the rewards of obedience.

One of the rewards of obedience is health. For too
long God's children have been double-minded concerning
God's will to heal. We have placed the "blame" on God
when a Christian got sick and died, murmuring, "It must
have been God's will."

On the other hand, we did give God the praise when
someone got well, especially from diseases that the world
considered terminal.

If you were on a jury at a trial and 30 witnesses who
were honest and upright men gave testimony the defendant
was innocent, but one witness said the defendant might be
guilty, what would your verdict be?

In my notebook I have 30 verses that speak of God's
will to heal us. Most people who say it is not God's will
to heal have one example from the Bible that they use in
their argument against healing, and that is Paul's thorn in
the flesh. It really can't be proven that Paul's thorn was a
sickness. In the Old Testament some "thorns" God spoke
about were people (Num. 33:55; Joshua 23:13; Judges
2:3).

The 30 verses in my notebook on healing do not
include any of the real life examples given in the gospels
where Jesus, who came to do the will of His Father,

healed people personally. Matthew 12:15 says, *"Many followed him, and he healed all their sick."* (The emphasis is mine.)

If you agree that Jesus spoke the truth when He said He came to do His Father's will (healing all their sick), then you should seriously question a belief that says it is not God's will to heal all when that is what Jesus did!

I challenge you to sincerely pray today's prayer and try to lay aside any negative teaching of your past. Please open up your spirit, heart and mind and let God reveal to you His will concerning healing.

Prayer: "Dear Father, I sincerely desire to understand Your will concerning healing. I pray that the eyes of my heart will be enlightened to see the truth about healing and health. Help me to lay aside any false teaching I may have had and sincerely seek truth.
"In Jesus' Name, Amen."

Today's Scripture Reading: Matt.8:1-17; John 6:36-38

Week 14 Day 2
Healing Through the Word

My son, pay attention to what I say; listen closely to my words. Do not let them out of your sight, keep them within your heart; for they are life to those who find them and health to a man's whole body. Proverbs 4:20-22

Sometimes someone who is ill seeks for a "miracle" of healing by going to a special faith healer for prayer. There is nothing wrong with this and many times an instantaneous healing does take place. Other times it does not. I'm not sure why this is so, but if you've had special prayer for healing and as yet do not see the results in

14

your body, do not despair.

There are other ways of healing. The verses in Proverbs 4 tell us that God's Word, when it becomes a part of our very being, is life and health to us. The truth of God's Word, when applied with faith and persistence, overcomes illness.

Most of you reading this book probably know, beyond a shadow of a doubt, that you are saved or born again. And if, on a certain day, you are depressed or worrying about something and not feeling "up" spiritually and someone asks you if you are saved, you certainly would answer "yes." That's what your answer would be since your salvation is based on what God's Word says and not on your feelings.

If you will, you can apply the same thing to healing. What does the Word say? *"God sent forth His Word and healed them (Ps. 107:20)"* and *"...by His wounds you have been healed (I Peter 2:24)."* The Word is Truth. Truth stays the same. Illness is a false thing which is subject to change. Illness changes from day to day. The Truth does not. On which do you wish to base your life (and health)?

Prayer: **"Dear Father, please help me to base my life, in all areas, on Your Truth. As an act of my will I choose to walk in the ways of truth.**
"In Jesus' Name, Amen."

Today's Scripture Reading: Psalms 107

Week 14 Day 3
A Healing Miracle

... by His wounds you have been healed. I Peter 2:24

15

I have a friend whose story I'd like to relate. In November of 1981, the doctors told her she would not live until Christmas. She had, in about a four-month period of time, seven serious surgeries because of kidney problems, none of which had been successful. In desperation she went from doctor to doctor. At last she found a Christian doctor who said he would operate. He suggested she pray and ask her friends to pray.

Lea agreed. She knew two prayers which were, "Now I lay me down to sleep" and part of the Lord's Prayer, so she said these and called five friends to pray.

In December, while in surgery, she died. Her spirit left her body, but as many say happens, she could still see her body and the operating room. She saw the surgeon remove his gloves, throw them on the floor and heard him say, "She's dead."

Then Lea saw a light at the end of a long tunnel, and out of the light came a "silent" voice saying, "Walk in the Word." This was "said" three times. Then she sat up on the operating table and said, "I don't know about you guys, but I'm not finished. Let's get this over!"

After surgery she asked her husband, "What do you think that means, 'Walk in the Word'?" He said he thought it meant to read the Bible. So she did. One evening she read I Peter 2:24.

She said to her husband, "This says, *'By His stripes I am healed.'* If the Word says I am healed, I must be healed, so I'm going to claim it. Will you agree with me?" He agreed to do that rather casually (as he was watching T.V. at the time).

So Lea began to say, *"By His stripes I am healed."* She continued to say it over and over and over. She quit taking medication and refused to talk to people who wouldn't agree and believe with her.

By now Lea had more problems than just her kidneys. Part of one kidney had been removed and an artificial tube had been put between the right kidney and the bladder. Muscles, nerves and her right hip bone had been

16

damaged, so she was unable to use her right leg and couldn't walk without great pain. The radioactive dyes and X-rays that had been given her repeatedly over 200 times caused her fingernails, toenails and patches of her hair to fall out. She was unable to eat any solid food and was on a liquid diet. She was in constant pain. Yet she said, hour after hour, day after day, *"By His stripes I am healed."*

In February of 1982, Lea was scheduled for some more X-rays. As she was in the dressing cubicle, she felt a warmth in her toes. Looking down she discovered her toenails were grown back. The warmth came up through her whole body.

When the X-rays were taken, the one kidney was whole and both were healed. The artificial tube in her bladder was gone, and even the internal scars from the surgeries did not show on the X-rays! Her fingernails and her hair were completely restored (and she had long hair). On the way home she stopped to eat a large meal at a restaurant. She could eat anything she desired!

I met her about a month after this and she walked, with no limp whatsoever, in high heels.

Lea used one verse and applied its truth until sickness and death were defeated in her life. Just as all the darkness in the world cannot put out the light of one little candle, neither could satan's lies to Lea put out the one small statement of truth to which she steadfastly held!

Prayer: **"Father, I thank You that Your Word is true and that You act upon it when I use it. Thank You that Jesus' stripes are still powerful today for the healing of Your people, for He is the same yesterday, today and forever.**
"Praise the Lord! Amen."

Today's Scripture Reading: I Peter 2

Week 14 Day 4
Healing From Illness

The Lord will sustain him on his sickbed and restore him from his bed of illness. Psalm 41:3

There are times when Christians do get ill. I believe this is not God's perfect will for us, but as yet most of us have not learned to always walk perfectly in redemption and righteousness.

I had a couple of colds in the last four months. How did this happen? The door was opened for the first one because I was negligent in the physical realm and got too tired and overworked. For the second cold, I opened the door through frustration and discouragement. Neither of those situations were God's best for me nor were the colds which resulted.

So, if you find yourself still sick sometimes, don't condemn yourself or blame God. Immediately apply yourself to restoration of health. When I am sick I still confess divine health and soon I have it again.

Since I have become fully convinced about God's will to heal, I have received healing completely from migraine headaches, which I had had for years. I have been healed of bladder infections and from a lump in my breast that the doctor said would have to be removed surgically. One time I fell off a chair onto our cement garage floor with the full impact of the fall on my left knee. I rebuked pain, confessed healing and continued cleaning the garage. I ended up with only a small black and blue spot on my knee.

You may say that those were all sort of minor things. What about something serious? My belief is that when people trust God for healing and see Him work in relatively minor things, they are built up in their faith. Then if something more serious comes along, they will be able to overcome it with their strong faith in God to heal.

Prayer: "Dear Lord, help me to trust You daily for health in my body. Teach me how to walk in complete wholeness.
"In Jesus' Name, Amen."

Today's Scripture Reading: Psalms 41 and 42

Week 14 Day 5
Conditions for Healing

Do not be wise in your own eyes; fear the Lord and shun evil. This will bring health to your body and nourishment to your bones. Proverbs 3:7, 8

There are several factors that enter into the picture of our health and healing. We need to depend on God's wisdom and not our own. This means we base our faith for healing firmly on God's Word, not looking at the illness or health of the Christians around us.

I know a lady who has been in poor health for many years. When I talk to her about healing, she is quick to tell me how her brother who had cancer and had been prayed for wasn't healed and died. Her doubt is based on her brother's experience.

My mother died of complications from cancer about five years ago. We had prayed and believed for her healing. But, I refuse to base my belief on my mother's experience, although she had been a Christian since childhood. My faith is firmly established in God's Word and I know His perfect will is healing for His children.

One does not need to be sick to die. When your spirit leaves your body, you die. You do not have to be ill for this to happen.

Why then, you may be asking, do so many Christians die from sickness? I believe it is because their churches don't teach that it is God's will to heal. Some churches do not teach salvation. Consequently, very few people in those churches are born again. It is certainly God's will that all be saved, but if people are not told about it, they don't know to receive it. The same principle applies to healing.

To walk in divine health we must shun evil. Don't smoke a pack of cigarettes a day for 30 years and then blame God when lung cancer is the result. Don't walk in unforgiveness and bitterness for 30 years and blame God when you develop heart trouble. If you have had "spiritual heart trouble" for years, don't be surprised when you begin to see it physically!

God's Word shows the way to forgiveness, peace and joy. If we deliberately, or in ignorance, do not walk in God's ways, consequences will follow, often showing up in our physical bodies. Don't let satan defeat you through illness. Learn to walk in the fear (respect, honor and awe) of the Lord. Respecting the Lord means you seek out and walk in His ways. Then His healing and love is free to flow into you spiritually, mentally and physically.

Prayer: "Lord, teach me to walk in Your ways concerning healing and health. I now see it is Your will to heal me.

"Lord, I choose to receive healing in my body from this day forward.

"In Jesus' Name, Amen."

Today's Scripture Reading: Psalm 119:88-104

Week 14 Day 6
Healing is God's Will

You will come to the grave in full vigor, like sheaves gathered in season. Job 5:26

When I talk with people who do not believe it is always God's will to heal, they often say, "Well, everyone has to die" as though that statement settles the argument, but it doesn't.

Not everyone has died. Enoch and Elijah didn't. Of course, unless the second coming occurs first, probably all of us will die. My contention is that you do not have to be sick to die. When the spirit leaves the body, at that point one is dead. You do not have to be sick for this to take place. Your spirit can leave your body without your having cancer, pneumonia or some other disease.

Then there is the favorite excuse of unhealed Christians, Paul's thorn in the flesh. "Thorns in the side" are mentioned in Numbers 33:55 and Joshua 23:13 in the Old Testament and they were people, not any physical ailment.

Also, Paul said his thorn was a *"messenger of satan."* He knew it wasn't from God. The Greek word "aggelas", means "angel (messenger) of satan." This root word is represented 186 times in the Bible and is never translated as disease or physical infirmity.

Even if Paul's thorn was illness, does it make sense to base your "belief" about healing on one scripture rather than on the multitude of scriptures that tell about healing?

Look up the death accounts of the Old Testament saints. The Word doesn't say they died of illness. In fact, when Moses died at 120 years of age, Deut. 34:5-7 says that his eyes weren't dimmed or his strength lessened.

Lastly, some people seem to always have a story about a friend or family member who was a wonderful Christian but died of some dread disease, or is living still in an unhealed condition.

If I based my belief of what God's will is on what other Christians do, say or are, I would be in a real mess -- and so will you if you do that. God's will must be based on what His Word says. Psalm 103:3 says, *"He...heals all my diseases!"*

Prayer: "Lord, help me base my faith on Your Word and not on circumstances or people.

Your Word is Truth. I will let your Word be light to my path and I will walk in it.
"In Jesus' Name, Amen."

Today's Scripture Reading: Psalm 103

Week 14 Day 7
Healing Light

Then your light will break forth like the dawn, and your healing will quickly appear;... Isaiah 58:8

You have been exposed to the light concerning healing because I have given you God's Word about it. Maybe some of this is new to you so it is just in its "dawning stage."

In the past, you may not have been speaking according to God's Word for health and healing. To walk in this new light, you must begin to speak correctly. If you say you are catching a cold or coming down with the flu, no doubt you will get what you say.

When you walk in the Word consistently so that your spirit knows and your mind believes that the Lord will keep you free from every disease (Deut. 7:15), and you then discipline your mouth to say healing and health scriptures, your healing will quickly appear!

Decide to make these Word based confessions every day for the rest of your life. I have made scriptures about health and healing a part of what I say during my daily prayer time every morning. I thank God that Christ's light is in me completely healing my spirit, heart, mind and body. I then quote verses on healing. They vary from day to day, and I praise and thank God as I quote them. I have found that the Word is life to me and health to my whole body!

I mention specific areas of my body that need special help, also. For instance, I used to have frequent

22

headaches. Knowing blood flow affects this, I now confess, "Thank You, Lord, that my blood flows through my body in perfect order and harmony." Now the headaches are greatly diminished, usually occuring only when I've been unwise by not caring properly for my physical body.

Prayer: "Dear Father, I see in Your Word it is Your will to heal me. I ask that this Word go down into my spirit and heart and begin that healing today. May the eyes of my heart be enlightened concerning divine health.
"In Jesus' Name, Amen."

Today's Scripture Reading: Luke 9:1-11

You can start today, if you haven't already, walking in health. (Please see the foreword to this book for an explanation of the correct way to use affirmations.) Here is the affirmation you can say:

"Christ's light is in me completely healing my spirit, heart, mind and body. I walk in divine health."

Look up these scriptures and choose at least three that speak to you and fit your situation: Ex. 15:26, 23:25, 26; Deut. 7:15, 30:20; Job 5:26; Psalm 30:2, 3, 41:3, 103:2, 3, 107:20, 119:37, 92, 93, 122; Prov. 3:7, 8, 4:20-23, 12:18, 14:30, 15:30, 16:24, 17:22; Is. 57:19, 58:8; Jer. 17:14, 30:17, 33:6; Mal. 4:2; Matt. 8:17; Luke 11:36; I Pet. 2:24; III John 2

Note: Names of individuals used in this book have been changed to protect their privacy.

Week 15
Prosperity

Week 15 Day 1
Is Prosperity God's Will?

Beloved, I pray that you may prosper in every way and [that your body] may keep well, even as [I know] your soul keeps well and prospers. III John 2 AMP

There has been much disagreement and discussion about whether or not God wants His people to have an abundance of money and/or earthly possessions. Again, if we are to know the correct answer, we must look at scripture, rather than the financial situations of Christian people.

Note that the scripture says, *"...prosper in every way."* I am sure this scripture means that we should prosper financially as well as in other areas of our lives.

II Corinthians 9:11 says, *"You will be made rich in every way so that you can be generous on every occasion..."* To be generous on every occasion, we need something to give. How many times have you desired to give, but have been unable to do so because of your financial lack? For most Christians this has been far too common an occurence!

God desires that we be liberal in our giving to others and to the spreading of His gospel. One of the main things that is preventing the gospel from going to all nations is the lack of funds!

Christians have thought for a long time that money was evil, but the Word says in I Tim. 6:10, *"The love of money (or greed) is the root of evil."* In Matt. 6:33 Jesus says we should seek first the kingdom of God and His righteousness; then all these things (and He was talking about material things) would be added to us.

Many Christians have experienced financial lack for years. I believe the reason is because their priorities have been incorrect and they have lacked knowledge concerning God's will and ways in the area of financial prosperity.

This week I will endeavor to help you see what God's ways are for prosperity. I pray you will have wisdom and discernment as you study this, for Proverbs 8:18 says, *"With me (wisdom) are riches and honor, enduring wealth and prosperity."*

Prayer: **"Father, please help me lay aside any misconceptions and false beliefs I have had concerning money, wealth or prosperity. Renew my mind and help me to understand what Your ways are in the area of finance.**

"Please help me to walk in correct financial stewardship guided by Your Spirit Who was sent to guide me into all truth.

"In Jesus' Name, Amen."

Today's Scripture Reading: Deut. 28:1-47

Week 15 Day 2
Stewardship

He who is faithful in a very little [thing], is faithful also in much; and he who is dishonest and unjust in a very little [thing], is dishonest and unjust also in much. Therefore, if you have not been faithful in the [case of] the unrighteous mammon -- the deceitful riches, money, possessions -- who will entrust to you the true riches? Luke 16:10, 11 AMP

God is looking for totally honest and wise stewards that He can trust with riches. Too many Christians are not faithful over little things. They block God's ability to bless them because they are not trustworthy with what money they now possess.

Search your heart today to make sure you are completely honest in all financial dealings. If the cashier gives you too much change, do you return the extra?

Do you steal from your employer? Do you steal from God? In the third chapter of Malachi, the people of Israel were cursed because they did not bring their tithes and offerings to the storehouse (God's temple).

If you are at all dishonest regarding financial matters, it shows that you have given money too high a priority in your life. Money has become an idol, because it is more important to you than an open and clear relationship with God!

If this is true, you are going to have to repent, change your ways, and put dollars in their proper place. This includes the things that money can buy, such as new cars and clothes.

I heard a story which I think will illustrate my point. A lady was involved in an accident in her husband's new car. She was very concerned about what his reaction would be. On pulling out the registration papers, she found this message written by her husband. "In case of accident, remember honey, it is you I love and not the car."

That man had his priorities straight! Too many of us put money, houses, cars, and things above people (God's top priority creation) and even above God Himself.

Please check your priorities today and ask God to help you put them in proper order.

Prayer: "Father, I repent of any dishonesty in my life. I repent of greed and the love of money and material possessions. I repent of being a poor steward of the money you have given me.

"I ask that You would bless me with

honesty. I desire to seek and put first Your kingdom.

"Please give me wisdom and prudence in money matters. I determine to be a good and honest steward from this day forward.

"Thank You, Father, for I pray in Your Son's Name, Who is made unto me Wisdom from You, Amen."

Today's Scripture Reading: Luke 16:10-13

Affirmation: "I am a wise steward. I always put God and His kingdom first in my life. Money is in proper perspective."

Affirmation Scriptures: Ps. 49:20; 62:10; Prov. 3:6 (LB); Matt. 6:33; Luke 12:15; 16:13; I Tim. 6:8, 10; Phil. 4:6; James 4:2.

Week 15 Day 3
Stewardship (Continued)

In everything you do put God first and He will direct you and crown your efforts with success. Proverbs 3:6 LB

In God's Word there are many good promises concerning the wealth and prosperity that our Father God desires to give to His children. So many have "claimed" these promises, but have not seen the actual material fruit in their lives. Often they have become discouraged, doubtful and upset with themselves or with God.

God cannot answer their prayers because they are not based on His ways. God cannot bless greedy people who are poor stewards. He must see the fruit of honesty, generosity and stewardship before He knows one can be trusted with wealth.

Proverbs 8:18 says, *"With wisdom are riches and honor, enduring wealth and prosperity. "* Proverbs 9:10 (AMP) says, *"The reverent and worshipful fear of the Lord is the beginning [the chief and choice part] of Wisdom and the knowledge of the Holy One is insight and understanding."*

This is the foundational teaching that I believe too many "prosperity preachers" have failed to teach in their messages.

God does watch over His Word to perform it (Jeremiah 1:12), but it must be confessed by people who have pure hearts and correct motives. It must be confessed by people who are wise in God's ways, who not only know His ways, but are also walking and living daily in those ways.

Many Christians are gullible when it comes to "get rich quick" schemes, of preachers who teach "worldly wisdom" concerning financial things. They are too easily persuaded to go along with someone's ideas on how they can make a lot of money to "give to God."

It seems as though satan easily deceives us when it comes to his lies in areas of finance. We must have God's wisdom established in our hearts to defeat the devil!

Prayer: **"Dear Lord, please give me supernatural wisdom in Your ways concerning money and finance, and help me to consistently walk in that wisdom. May I not be put off balance in material things by any of satan's deceits.**

"I pledge myself to renew my mind by using Your Word and knowing Your ways concerning money in my life.

"In Jesus' Name, Amen."

Today's Scripture Reading: Luke 12:15-34

Week 15 Day 4
Being Debt Free

The Lord shall open to you His good treasury, the heavens to give the rain of your land in its season, and to bless all the work of your hand; and you shall lend to many nations, but you shall not borrow. Deuteronomy 28:12 AMP

Many Christians are hindered in their service to the Lord because of financial difficulties. Many are in deep debt, and instead of being able to easily give God 10% tithe, they are having to pay 12% to 20% interest to banks, loan companies or stores where they have credit cards.

I am so thankful that years ago I broke up and threw away my credit cards from the department stores! I thus avoided hundreds of dollars interest by paying cash for clothes, furniture, etc.

Phil. 4:19 says that my God will supply all my needs, not Penny's, Sears, or K-Mart!

Proverbs 13:22 says the wealth of the wicked is to come to the righteous. For a long time the opposite has been happening and the Christians have been paying excessive interest to the worldly financial systems. It is time to stop that negative backward flow. I know it can be done. More and more Christians are becoming debt free!

Some seem to think being in debt is a sin. I don't see it as sin but I do see it as living below the privileges and blessings God wants to provide for us.

You may be buried under a huge amount of bills and debts. God wants you free from that! You may see no way out, but as you learn to confess correctly and begin to walk in God's ways concerning finance, you will begin to see God work for you.

Just last night I asked a young single friend of mine where she was living now. She shared that she had recently been able to buy her own home. The elderly man selling his place had actually paid the closing costs because he wanted a Christian to have the house.

God has many creative ideas. Look to <u>Him</u> as your source and not your employers, banks or worldly institutions. Depend on God first!

Prayer: "Lord, I want to learn to depend on You as my source. As I walk in Your ways I know I will open avenues so that You can meet my needs and bless me financially. Continue to bless me with good stewardship and wisdom. "In Jesus' Name, Amen."

Today's Scripture Reading: Psalm 35:18-28 and Psalm 128

Affirmation: "I am debt free and know how to live in financial freedom to the praise and glory of God."

Affirmation Scriptures: Josh. 1:8, Job 8:7, Ps. 106:4, 5, 35:27, 128:l, 2, 72:7; Prov. 13:21, 22, 10:22; Jer. 31:14, 32:42, 44.

Week 15 Day 5
God is Your Source

And my God will liberally supply (fill to the full) your every need according to His riches in glory in Christ Jesus. Philippians 4:19 AMP

Each day we need to believe and expect that all of our needs will be taken care of by God. God is our source; not the government with food stamps and social security checks; not our employer with a pay check; not a wealthy relative from whom we can borrow money, but God! God may use all of these things to supply our needs, but as His children we need to look to Him as our true source. Seeing God as our real supplier will help us stand firm when financial adversities come.

About three years ago a "friend" said he would buy a home for us. Acting on that man's word, we signed papers and moved into the house he had agreed to buy. About the time we moved in, Mr. J. said, "No deal." Derin and I decided that our source was not Mr. J. but God!

Through great duress we stood firm on our confession that God was our source. Up to the closing time no money came in for the purchase of the house. For eight long days after the closing, none came in.

We did not go from person to person or bank to bank seeking funds. We prayed and confessed the Word. One Sunday, nine days later, a lady whom we didn't know personally, said to a friend of ours, "If the Carmacks had not moved, we could have helped them." Our friend said, "They haven't moved."

That afternoon Mr. & Mrs. W. came to our home and told us they would provide all of the money for us to buy the house, and they did! God supplied our need because we steadfastly depended on Him to do it!

Many Christians are double-minded in the area of finance. You must know what the Word says concerning God, money and prosperity. Then you must get the truth firmly entrenched in your heart and mind. This will cause you not to waver or doubt. James 1:6 &7 says that one who doubts and wavers cannot receive anything from the Lord.

Prayer: **"Father God, You are my Father and You do supply my needs. It is not Your will that I have unmet needs and lack in my life. Please show me the areas where I need to change in my beliefs, thinking, money habits and my confession. I desire to become single-minded in the area of finance.**

"Help me not to block, in any way, the supply that You want to provide for me. Give me strong faith in Your desire for prosperity for me.

"In Jesus' Name, Amen."

Today's Scripture Reading: Phil. 4:10-19

Affirmation: "I know God's ways concerning finance, and am single-minded in believing His ways. His blessing is on my life. He supplies all my needs."

Affirmation Scriptures: Job 22:21; Ps. 86:11; II Cor. 8:9; 9:8, 9:11; Phil. 4:19; Heb. 10:23; 13:5; James 1:5-8.

Week 15 Day 6
Sowing and Reaping

...he who sows righteousness reaps a sure reward.
Proverbs 11:18

God is a God of miracles. The Bible illustrates many accounts of miraculous provision by the Lord, and miracles are still happening today. However, most of the time I believe God provides according to the laws of nature that He has set up.

When a gardener sows beans, he doesn't pray for and expect corn for the crop. When I plant peas in mid-April, I don't expect to be picking and eating them by May 1. Nature's laws of sowing and reaping are not set up that way!

When Christians sow poor stewardship and negative words in the financial area of their lives, they shouldn't expect a "miracle crop" of financial blessing. We have been upset with God because He hasn't answered our pleas for instant cash, when we should have, been examining our own attitudes and habits in giving, and our confessions about receiving.

Some people don't "plant" tithes, offerings and gifts to God and yet they expect a harvest. Others give or plant faithfully, but they "water" their planting with negative words and unbelief. In either case, their harvest will be destroyed by satan. If you are not doing things God's way, His hands are tied and He cannot bless you!

Not only must Christians learn mentally God's laws concerning finance, but they must also establish in their hearts the right belief, the knowing of God's ways concerning finance and then walk in those ways. Then God is free to accomplish His will for them materially, which, according to Jeremiah 31, is bounty, prosperity and restoration of fortunes.

God has set up a time for sowing and reaping, seed time and harvest and laws governing it. We must ask for and receive knowledge and wisdom to observe those laws. Then His will to bless us with abundance can be accomplished.

Prayer: "Lord, teach me Your ways concerning giving and receiving, sowing and reaping.

"Lord, help me to plant wisely and harvest faithfully. Please give me wisdom and knowledge to be a faithful steward of the riches you desire for me to receive. I pledge that I will become knowledgeable in the area of finance so satan can't destroy me through money problems (Hosea 4:6).

"In Jesus' Name, Amen."

Today's Scripture Reading: Prov. 11:18-12:14 (Read, underline and note all the ways that a righteous man is rewarded materially.)

Week 15 Day 7
Receiving Abundance

And God is able to make all grace (every favor and earthly blessing) come to you in abundance, so that you may always and under all circumstances and whatever the need, be self-sufficient -- possessing enough to require no aid or support and furnished in abundance for every good work and charitable donation. II Corinthians 9:8 AMP

According to this scripture God desires that we have favor and earthly blessing in abundance. In the dictionary abundance means "amply sufficient, great plenty."

We are not only to have enough for ourselves and our family, but also we are to have an abundance in order to give to good works (effective ministries that are spreading the gospel) and charities (organizations that are helping the poor).

I have talked with many Christians who wanted to have this abundance and be able to give, but their finances were still lacking and they had trouble even meeting their own needs. God wants to see that changed. There is no lack in heaven or with God Himself! The blockage is somewhere between God and us.

Here are some things you can do to change the financial picture in your life.

Pray this prayer (adding specifics as needed): "Lord, I repent of greed and the love of money and material things. Take greed out of my heart and bless me with a spirit of generosity and giving. As an act of my will I put God and His kingdom first in my life.

"Forgive me, Lord, for all dishonesty. (Confess specifics here if need be.) I will repay those I've cheated or stolen from, and from now on I will walk in utmost integrity.

"Lord, I have been ignorant and

unenlightened about Your will, as revealed in Your Word, concerning money. I will study and meditate in the Word concerning money and wealth so I won't be destroyed for lack of knowledge (Hosea 4:6).

"I ask that You renew my mind and give me wisdom in understanding Your financial principles.

"Forgive me, Lord, for robbing You by not paying my tithes. Starting with this pay check, I will tithe <u>first,</u> knowing You will meet all my needs when I give to You.

"God, You love a cheerful giver, so I will give to You with joy in my heart, knowing You will provide an abundance for all my needs.

"Lord, change my heart and renew my mind according to Your Word and Your will. Then my heart will be in the right attitude to receive from You.

"Take all selfishness and bitterness out of my heart. As an act of my will, I forgive everyone who has stolen from me and/or cheated me in business dealings. I forgive those who owe money to me. I pledge to walk unselfishly and in forgiveness toward all people from this time forward.

"In the strong Name of Jesus, Amen."

Today's Scripture Reading: II Cor. 8:1-21, 9:6-15

Week 16
Getting Free From Fear

Week 16 Day 1
Overcoming Fear

Be strong and courageous. Do not be afraid...for the Lord your God goes with you; he will never leave you nor forsake you. Deuteronomy 31:6

If you have been living habitually in fear, you need to ask God to remove the fear and replace it with confidence, peace and faith. God can and will take fear out of your heart when you ask Him to do it. It will then be up to you to renew your mind so that when satan tempts you to be fearful again, you can overcome him by using God's Word.

This week you will be given prayers, verses, scripture passages and practical ideas that can lead you out of fear, worry and anxiety. They can be replaced with an attitude of confidence and security in God's love.

Prayer: **"Dear Father, I don't even remember or know all the things that happened in my childhood and adult years that caused me to become fearful, but You do. I am praying right now and asking You, with the light of Jesus Christ, Your Son, to heal all those hurts in my spirit and heart and, with the blood of Jesus, wash all my fears away. Please replace them with peace, confidence, tranquility and perfect trust in You, God. "Help me be faithful and persistent as I renew my mind and learn to "fix my mind" on what is good.**
"In Jesus' Name, Amen."

Today's Scripture Reading: Is. 32:17-20

Confess: "God has set me free from fear. I walk in confidence and faith. I have inner peace."

Affirmation Scriptures: Deut. 31:6; Ps. 27:1, 3, 94:19-(LB), 112:7; Prov. 14:30; Is. 12:2, 32:17, 40:10; John 14:27; Rom. 8:15; Eph. 3:12; Phil. 4:6, 1:6; Col. 3:15; II Tim. 1:7; Heb. 4:16, 10:35, 36.

Week 16 Day 2
Freedom from Fear

For God did not give us a spirit of ... fear -- but [He has given us a spirit] of power and of love and of calm and well-balanced mind and discipline and self-control. II Timothy 1:7 AMP

I have been in discussion groups where it was questioned whether or not fear was a sin. I'm not going to try to convince you it is or is not. I do know that God has provided a way out of fear and I believe He wants us to walk in peace and confidence.

Fear, and its companions (timidity, cowardice, worry, anxiety and shyness), indicate a lack of trust and faith in God and His promises and/or ignorance of who you are in Christ Jesus.

Many people are fearful of condemnation from God. They have had teaching that God is a fearsome judge watching and waiting to "get them" for any sins or mistakes.

True, Proverbs 9:10 says, *"The fear of the Lord is the beginning of wisdom ..."* The Hebrew root for the word "fear" means 'to stand in awe and show reverence.' (It also can mean to be afraid or have fear of God if you are not walking in His ways.)

38

Let me tell you, if I were not born again and my sins taken away by the precious blood of Jesus, I would certainly have fear about God's judgment. So if you are an unforgiven sinner, it would be wise to fear God and quickly get into a right relationship with Him. Here's how to pray:

Prayer: "Father, I have sinned and rebelled against Your ways. I ask that You forgive me and by the blood of Jesus, cleanse away my guilt. I repent and turn away from my sins and I accept Your forgiveness. I accept Jesus as my Saviour. I confess that Jesus Christ is the Son of God and I choose to make Him the Lord of my life from this day forward.
"In Jesus' Name I pray, Amen."

Today's Scripture Reading: Romans 8:1-17

Confess: **"I am born again. God has forgiven my sins by the blood of Jesus. I stand before God without fear, guilt or condemnation."**

Week 16 Day 3
The Father's Love

For you did not receive a spirit that makes you a slave again to fear, but you received the Spirit of sonship. And by him we cry, "Abba , Father." Romans 8:15

God intended that our fathers be examples of love, protection and godliness, giving us an understanding of His love, protection and holiness. It is a very sad situation that satan has been so effective in causing fathers not to be the spiritual leaders they should be in their homes.

Some, like myself, have had the wonderful blessing of a godly father, and in my case, a godly grandfather, also. They were examples to me of love, protection and godliness. I remember when there were winter blizzards, my Daddy would come to our country school and walk ahead of me all the way home, guiding me and breaking the force of the wind and blowing snow. That was sacrificial love. That was protection and security.

I pray that the daddies who read this will realize the significance of their God-given responsibility and today make a quality decision to be the kind of fathers God would have them to be. Then their children will be so much better able to comprehend God's love, and as they believe and receive His love, they can live without fear!

This is my prayer for fathers: (If you are a dad, please change it to make it personal.)

Prayer: "Lord, I pray for the dads today. Help them to be the spiritual leaders in their homes. Let them express love and give security to their wives and children. May they strive to walk perfectly before You. Lord, take selfishness and anger from their hearts and help them to be the godly examples their families need to see.
"In Jesus' Name, Amen."

Today's Scripture Reading: Eph. 5:25, 6:4; Col. 3:19-21; I Tim. 3:1-7. (Read these in the Amplified Bible if possible.)

Week 16 Day 4
The Father's Love (Continued)

There is no fear in love -- dread does not exist; but full-grown (complete, perfect) love turns fear out of doors and expels every trace of terror! I John 4:18 AMP

God has perfect love toward us. If only we could fully comprehend that love, we would not be fearful at all!

Perfect love wants us to walk in divine health (Deut. 7:15). Perfect love desires that all our needs be met with enough left over so we can joyfully give to others (II Cor. 9:8, 11). Perfect love sends angels to protect us (Ps. 91:11). Perfect love comforts our hurting hearts (Jer. 31:13).

Every good and perfect gift is from our Father above Who does not change (James 1:17). His love is unconditional. I John 4:16a (AMP) says, *"And we know (understand, recognize, are conscious of, by observation and by experience), and believe (... put faith in and rely on) the love God cherishes for us."*

So many times we have blamed God for the bad or tragic happenings in our lives. On the other hand, we took the credit from God and gave it to "luck" for the good things!

Three things that block the good from happening are ignorance, unbelief and double-mindedness. Eliminate these three things by diligently reading, memorizing, meditating on and applying God's Word. You will then know how to reach out and receive the blessings God so earnestly desires for you.

If you will establish in your heart and mind (become single-minded about the following fact), it will change your life. Satan comes to kill, steal and destroy. Jesus, who came to earth as a gift from the Father, wants us to have an <u>abundant</u> life (John 10:10).

Prayer: "Dear Lord, please forgive me for being ignorant of Your ways. Help me to get rid of doubt and establish faith, belief and single-mindedness in my life. Help me to know Your Word and <u>do</u> it, using it every day in all situations of my life.

"In Jesus' Name, Amen."
Today's Scripture Reading: James 1

41

Week 16 Day 5
Steps to Freedom

Do not be anxious about anything, but in everything, by prayer and petition, with thanksgiving, present your requests to God. And the peace of God, which transcends all understanding, will guard your hearts and your minds in Christ Jesus. Finally, brothers, whatever is true, ...noble, ...right, ...pure, ...lovely, ...admirable, -- if anything is excellent or praiseworthy -- think about such things. Philippians 4:6-8

There are three steps in this portion of scripture. They are your steps to being free of fear.

The first step is to pray a definite prayer with thanksgiving and praise, asking God to remove fear, being specific about any fears you have (v. 6).

Secondly, let those fears and anxieties be replaced with a peace that will guard your heart and mind (v. 7).

Thirdly, take control of your mind and concentrate only on good thoughts (v. 8). These three steps can be accomplished by the process given above and by praying this prayer or one that is similar:

Prayer: "Dear Father, I come to You in Jesus' Name. I ask forgiveness for letting fear have control in my life. I ask You, my loving Heavenly Father, to remove fear from my life. Take out all fear of_____(name your specific fears here).

"Please replace those fears with peace and confidence. Teach me to walk unafraid in Your freedom.

"Thank You for setting me free from fear.

"In Jesus' Name, Amen."

Today's Scripture Reading: Hebrews 4

Use the confession given earlier this week to change the fear pattern to a confidence and peace pattern. Give the Holy Spirit control of your mind. Daily cast down fear and quote scriptures such as Romans 8:5 which says, *"The mind controlled by the Spirit is life and peace."* Quote them until they are a very part of your inner being. Then you can be free of fear.

Week 16 Day 6
Conquering Fear

For the law of the Spirit of life [which is] in Christ Jesus [the law of our new being], has freed me from the law of sin and of death. Romans 8:2 AMP

Many people are fearful because of the breakdown of our society. There is fear of robbery, assault and rape. There is fear of high blood pressure, heart attacks and cancer. There is fear of divorce, rebelling children and suicide. There is fear of military involvement and nuclear war.

A person can be consumed by these fears, or he/she can choose to find out his/her rights, blessings and authority in Christ and be an overcomer of fear.

I have no fear of assault or rape. I know that the power within me (Jesus) is greater than the power of the assailant (satan) coming against me (I John 4:4). Because of my authority in Jesus, I would never allow someone controlled by satan to harm me.

One of the reasons there is so much physical illness today is because of fear. Women are actually having their breasts removed before there is any sign of cancer because of fear! I persistently commanded the lump in my breast to leave (in Jesus' Name) until it was gone. That has been over three years ago and it has never come back.

When God's love and peace rule in our homes, the fear of family break-up leaves. The spirits of divorce, rebellion and suicide are defeated when love is in control of the family.

Together, as Christians, we must pray diligently for peace in our world. We must bless our leaders with wisdom. We need to repent of our national sins and pray there will be a great spiritual awakening world wide.

We need not fear death because we are ready to go home to heaven. How peaceful our lives can be when we know who we are in Christ!

Prayer: **"Father God, Your world and the people in it are longing for peace, safety and the manifestation of Your love and power. Help me to know who I am in Jesus and what my dominion is in Him.**

"Lord, Your acts are in response and answer to men's prayers and men speaking Your Word. Help me to pray and speak correctly so that as Matthew 6:10 says, 'Your kingdom come, Your will be done, on earth as it is in heaven.'

"In the powerful Name of Jesus, Amen."

Today's Scripture Reading: Romans 8:13-39

Week 16 Day 7
Conquering Fear (Continued)

If you make the Most High your dwelling -- even the Lord, ...then no harm will befall you, no disaster will come near your tent. Psalm 91: 9 & 10

How we desire to be free of the fear of harm or disaster! However, there is a condition we must meet. We must be <u>dwelling</u> in the Lord. He is to be our habitation, the place where we live, our home.

Our relationship with Him is not casual and fleeting but one of abiding in His presence at all times. We will communicate with Him in prayer; we will be aware of His presence; we will be listening to what He says and agreeing with it daily.

Deut. 7:15 says, *"The Lord will keep you free from every disease."* This wonderful promise was to those who kept His commands and laws (v. 11).

God's Word is filled with wonderful promises for His children, but there are conditions we must meet to be assured of receiving those promises.

So often Christians open the door to satan's destruction through disobedience and wrong confessions. Too often we speak what we don't really want instead of the truth of God's Word. Too often we are living parts of our lives in the "tents of wickedness" instead of dwelling in the righteousness of God in Christ Jesus.

We must seek to follow after God with our whole hearts, with single-minded desires and with disciplined bodies. Then we can expect and receive God's best for us.

Prayer: "Father, this week I have learned how to walk without fear in Your kingdom of light. Please help me to use this knowledge along with Your wisdom, walking in the truth and abiding in You.

"In Jesus' Name, Amen."

Today's Scripture Reading: Psalm 91 (Amplified Bible if you have one)

Week 17
The Word

Week 17 Day 1
The Power of the Word

Every scripture is God breathed -- given by His inspiration -- and profitable for instruction, for reproof and conviction of sin, for correction of error and discipline in obedience and for training in righteousness [that is, in holy living, in conformity to God's will in thought, purpose and action] so that the man of God may be complete and proficient, well-fitted and thoroughly equipped for every good work. II Timothy 3:16 & 17 AMP

Christians have not realized the power and importance of God's Word. His Word is to be a part of our very being, established in our spirits, hearts and minds. It is to be our key to escaping temptation (Luke 4:1-14), preventing sin (Ps. 119:11), having health (Prov. 4:20-22), receiving prosperity (Joshua 1:8), getting answers to prayer (John 15:7), acquiring wisdom (Col. 3:16) and many other benefits.

Some people say that calamities or hard times come into their lives to bring them into a deeper walk with God. I do not believe that is so. I believe what really happens is that when we are not walking close to God, satan comes in and brings bad situations into our lives. Since we are Christians we seek God for help and He, in His compassion, helps us and this draws us closer to Him.

As today's verse says, God would much rather the Word would be our reproof, discipline and guide. The Word, firmly established in your life, will prevent many of life's trials, and when a trial does come, the Word will show you the way to overcome and be victorious in it!

47

Prayer: "Dear Lord, I have been neglecting Your precious Word. I ask Your forgiveness and I determine that I will spend time each day reading and confessing Your words for they truly are words of life.

"In the Name of the Word Who became flesh and lived among us (John 1:14), Amen."

Today's Scripture Reading: Ps. 19:7-11

Affirmation: "God's Word is vital in my life. I read it, memorize it, and meditate on it. I enjoy studying the Word because it is life to me."

Afffirmation Scriptures: Ps. 12:6, 19:7, 8, 119:93, 105, 138:2 (AMP); Prov. 22:17-19; Mark 13:31; Luke 1:37 (AMP), 8:15; John 14:26, 17:17; Acts 20:32; Rom. 10:8; Heb. 4:12, 8:10. Also, see the verses used or referred to in today's devotional.

Week 17 Day 2
Using the Word

...for You have exalted above all else Your name and Your word, and You have magnified Your word above all Your name! Psalm 138:2 AMP

This verse tells us what great importance God places on His Word. If we, too, will give His Word honor and importance in our lives, we will benefit greatly.

It distresses me to talk with Christians who do not know how to use the Word of God to defeat satan in their lives. I cannot condemn them because that is where I used to be when I lived an up and down, yo-yo type Christian experience.

Now, if satan tries to put anger, fear, depression or sickness on me, I instantly know what to do to defeat him. I defeat him with the words of my mouth by quoting scripture. That is what Jesus did in Luke 4. Satan's temptations were overcome by the quoting of scripture and Jesus was victorious!

We can be victorious over satan, also. Revelation 12:11 (AMP) says, *"And they have overcome (conquered) him* (meaning satan) *by the blood of the Lamb and by the utterance of their testimony ..."* Notice the word utterance. When you utter something, you say it out loud. It is good to silently quote scripture, but it is much more effective to say it out loud against satan's temptations! It also builds up your faith to hear the Word (Rom. 10:17).

Prayer: **"I pray, Lord, that Your Word will come alive in me and that I will understand how to use it to live victoriously. Help me to memorize it and meditate on it consistently, so that I am single-minded and have strong faith.** **"In Jesus' Name, Amen."**

Today's Scripture Reading: Ps. 119:1-32

Week 17 Day 3
Believing the Word

Listen [consent and submit] to the words of the wise, and apply your mind to my knowledge; for it will be pleasant if you keep them in your mind [believing them], your lips will be accustomed to [confessing] them. That your trust -- belief, reliance, support and confidence -- may be in the Lord. *Proverbs 22:17-19 AMP*

Satan loves to make people doubt God and the truth of His Word. Satan wants you to doubt your salvation.

He wants you to doubt God's goodness and to shake your faith in your fellow Christians.

This verse shows that your proper attitude toward the Word should be consenting and submitting to it and believing in it. This attitude, with the act of confessing it with your lips, will bring trust and confidence in the Lord.

So, to have stronger belief (faith) in God, study and know His Word. It is really quite simple, but expect a battle from satan when you decide to give the Word priority in your life.

Some of the devil's lies (which he has probably already tried to tell you) may be: "You're too busy." "You don't have time to read the Word." "You won't understand what you read." "The Bible is hard to read." "You can't memorize the Word." "The Bible was written for saints and special people like preachers or priests, not you."

You can overcome satan's lies by correct confession such as: "The Word has priority in my life." "I enjoy reading God's Word and I understand it." "It is easy for me to memorize the Word." Then cut out an hour a day of T.V. watching (even if it is Christian T.V.) and get into the study of God's Word!

Prayer: "Dear Lord, please help me give your Word the priority it deserves in my life. Help me to memorize it and use it daily. May the eyes of my heart be enlightened as I read and study it in order for it to become alive and powerful in my everyday life!
"In Jesus' Name, Amen."

Today's Scripture Reading: Ps. 119:33-72

Week 17 Day 4
Controlled by the Word

The word of God is living and active. Sharper than any double-edged sword, it penetrates even to dividing soul and spirit, joints and marrow; it judges the thoughts and attitudes of the heart. Hebrews 4:12

God's Word is not a history book of dead words that ancient man wrote. It is as true today as it was when the Holy Spirit inspired its writing. It is alive and effective.

After I started learning and using (being a doer of) the Word, I could tell the difference between what my mind was feeling and what my spirit was knowing. The Word helped me divide soul (mind) and spirit. The Word, established firmly in your spirit, will start controlling and guiding your mind.

Romans 8:6 says *"...the mind controlled by the Spirit is life and peace."* Our minds won't be controlled by the Holy Spirit unless our human spirits are first trained in and controlled by the Holy Spirit through God's Holy Scriptures. This is where single-mindedness comes in. To be single-minded, we must know a truth, both in our spirits and in our minds. So many Christians blame God for the circumstances of life that are hurtful or negative when the real reason their prayers aren't answered is because they are double-minded (see James 1:6-8). The cure for double-mindedness is to apply the Word daily, establish it in your mind and your spirit so you can no longer be tempted by life's circumstances or satan's lies to doubt God!

Prayer: "Lord, help me to establish the belief that Your Word is true in my mind and spirit so that I am single-minded and steadfast in my trust in You. Help me to memorize and use Your Word to establish Your will in my life. "In Jesus' Name, Amen."

Week 17 Day 5
Guided by the Word

Your Word is a lamp to my feet and a light for my path. Psalm 119:105

One of the things people often discuss or ask is, "What is God's will for me?" Romans 12:2 says that when you are transformed by the renewing of your mind, then you can prove for yourself what is God's will for you.

The best way, and probably the only one, to truly renew your mind is to use God's Word. Satan likes to set up patterns of negative thinking in our lives that, when followed often enough, become habitual ways of thought for us.

For many people, thoughts such as these have been with them for years and years: "I am ugly." "I am dumb." "I can't witness." "I am afraid." "People don't like me." All of these negative attitudes can be overcome by using the appropriate scriptures and saying them aloud daily (as I've taught you to do at the beginning of this book and in *Image to Image,* Volume I).

When you walk in the light of the truth of God's Word, satan sees that in you and it overpowers and dispels the darkness of his lies. When you walk in God's light, you can walk free of the hang-ups that have kept you from knowing and doing God's will in your life. This is a freedom satan does not want you to have but it is your decision. You can choose to walk in the Word and attain your freedom!

Prayer: "Dear Father God, I repent and turn from, and ask Your forgiveness for, the negative thoughts and habits I've had in my past. Please

help me to renew my mind by using the light and truth of Your Word. I want to know the truth and be set free by it (John 8:32).
"In the Light-giver's Name, Amen."

Today's Scripture Reading: Ps. 119:105-128

Week 17 Day 6
Abiding in the Word

If you live in Me -- abide vitally united to Me -- and My words remain in you and continue to live in your hearts, ask whatever you will and it shall be done for you. John 15:7 AMP

Christians often quote this verse as a promise that God will answer their prayers, that they can ask whatever they wish and God is obligated to do what they ask. But too many of them are not vitally united to Jesus. Legally, the people about which I am speaking are Christians. They have asked for forgiveness and accepted Jesus as their Saviour, but they really haven't made Him Lord in their lives.

Probably all of you know a couple who is legally married, but not vitally united in their relationship. If you will ponder the difference between legal and vital in a marriage relationship, you will understand what I am saying about the difference between legal and vital salvation.

Then there is the matter of the Word. It is supposed to <u>live</u> in our hearts and spirits. It takes more than just casually reading a chapter or two of the Bible each day for the Word to <u>live</u> in your heart.

When you hear the saying, "They know that by heart," that means that someone has memorized something thoroughly and knows it well.

53

If you asked the average group of Christians to quote by memory three scriptures they use to defeat satan (verses on health, joy, peace or patience) you would be amazed at how few in the crowd know even three verses in the area of their temptation!

Satan has some of you convinced you cannot memorize scripture. Do you know your name, address, phone number and birthdate? Then you can memorize scripture! Begin today confessing you can do it and then do it.

Prayer: "Lord, help me to understand what it is to abide in Jesus. Help me to memorize Your Word and use it daily to walk in victory over situations, temptations or problems in my life.

"In the Name of Jesus, in Whom I abide, Amen."

Today's Scripture Reading: Ps. 119:129-152

Week 17 Day 7
The Permanence of the Word

Heaven and earth will pass away, but my words will never pass away. Mark 13:31

God's words are established forever. The Word that you have within you today will be with you throughout eternity. That alone should inspire you to memorize and possess the Word in your heart. But the fact is that many have a hard time relating to heaven and eternity. What they want are answers for here and now, for daily problems in their lives. The Word has those answers, also! If you have fear, the Word has verses that tell you how to have confidence and peace. If you are bitter and angry, the

Word tells you how to walk in forgiveness and have self-control. If lust is a problem, there are verses on purity that you can use to renew your mind. All of the negative attitudes of guilt, inferiority, grief, despair, and rebellion have an answer in scripture.

Figure out the opposite of your problem, use a good concordance (you can buy one at a Christian bookstore), and look up the verses that will help you. Then use those verses daily against satan until you know you have victory in that area of your life. (Or you can order our *Scripture Cards*).

Prayer: **"Dear Lord, I desire that Your Word become a vital part of my life. Help me to use it to overcome all temptations from satan and negative or sinful areas of my personality. Help me to hide Your Word in my heart that I might not sin against You (Ps. 119:11).**
"In Jesus' Name, Amen."

Today's Scripture Reading: Ps. 119:153-176

Week 18
The Lord's Prayer

Week 18 Day 1
God The Father

Our Father Who is in Heaven, hallowed (kept holy) be Your name. Matthew 6:9 AMP

This week I want to look closely at the Lord's Prayer and see what is really in it. For years I prayed this prayer out loud in unison in church, giving almost no thought to its meaning.

Within this past year, I have been using the Lord's Prayer often as I take communion privately. I have gained some insights into it that I would like to share with you.

First, it is significant that Jesus would tell us to call God, our <u>Father</u>. Before Jesus came people who served God were called His servants. The disciples knew Jesus was God's Son, but by telling them to pray, *"Our Father,"* He was letting them know they were God's sons, also. As I John 3:1 says, so are you and I God's children! We need to cherish and remember that fact, always!

Next, this scripture establishes "where God is." He is in heaven, His holy dwelling place. From heaven He oversees all the happenings here on earth and is in control of what we give to Him.

His name is holy and we need to be careful to keep it holy. I hear even some Christians say, "O God!" They are using it as a slang expression. We need to be careful to give God's name the reverence and respect that it deserves. Certainly we should never use it in swearing or cursing.

Exodus 20:7 (AMP) says, *"You shall not use or repeat the name of the Lord your God in vain [that is,*

57

*lightly or frivolously, in false affirmations or profanely];
for the Lord will not hold him guiltless who takes His
name in vain."*

**Prayer: Each day this week pray the Lord's
Prayer slowly and thoughtfully.**

Today's Scripture Reading: Matt. 6:1-15

Week 18 Day 2
God's Kingdom

*...your kingdom come, your will be done, on earth as
it is in heaven. Matthew 6:10*

In Luke 17:21 (AMP) Jesus said, "*...the kingdom of
God is within you (in your hearts) and among you
(surrounding you)."* The first place to start seeing God's
will done on earth is within yourself. If there is anything
in your life that you don't feel is God's best for you, you
need to repent, turn from it and establish righteousness in
that area of your life.

Now consider what heaven is like: No sickness, no
sorrow, no poverty, no starving children, no disease, no
sin, no lust, no child abuse, no fear, no anger, no
bitterness or hatred. And we are praying that God's will
be done here on earth as it is in heaven!

I do not expect earth to become that perfect until satan
is bound for the 1,000 year reign of Christ here on earth
(Rev. 20:4). However, it is our privilege and duty, I
believe, to do our best to have God's will done in us and
in our families and homes. Our personal kingdom should
be a "bit of heaven" here on earth.

We can also fervently pray that more and more people
begin to live in that way. I personally pray that the people
of our nation will repent and have spiritual renewal. I pray
for the peace of Jerusalem and that the Jewish people will

realize Jesus is their Messiah. I pray we will have godly rulers in our government. Our prayers do make a difference in the world!

Prayer: The Lord's Prayer

Today's Scripture Reading: Luke 18:1-17

Week 18 Day 3
Daily Bread

Give us today our daily bread. Matthew 6:11

This verse can be taken literally with the request being that we are provided with our daily physical need for sustenance. Jesus said we didn't need to be concerned with what we would eat or wear because God knew of these needs. He tells us in Matt. 6:25-34 that He will provide for us when we seek first His kingdom and His righteousness.

This verse can be taken spiritually, also. In Matthew 4:4 Jesus said, *"Man does not live by bread alone, but on every word that comes from the mouth of God."* In John 6:35 Jesus said, *"I am the bread of life."* He had been trying to teach the disciples the difference between physical bread from heaven (manna) and spiritual Bread, the Bread of God, who was Jesus (verse 33).

Actually God wants us to have both physical and spiritual bread each day. And just as you would become weak and eventually die physically if you did not eat, so you will become weak and die spiritually if you do not feed your spirit with God's Word.

Another time that bread was of great significance was when Jesus served the Last Supper to His disciples (Luke 22:19). This is my own opinion (I can't prove it scripturally) but I have thought that perhaps "daily bread" means we are to take communion daily. Acts 2:46 (AMP) says of the believers, *"Day after day...in their homes they broke bread [including the Lord's Supper]."* Taking communion often has become a part of my life and I believe it has helped me grow spiritually.

I have heard that Smith Wigglesworth, who was a powerful preacher and saw many miracles in his ministry, took communion daily.

Prayer: The Lord's Prayer

Today's Scripture Reading: John 6:1-14, 22-40

Week 18 Day 4
Forgiveness

And forgive us our debts, as we also have forgiven (left, remitted and let go the debts and given up resentment against) our debtors. Matthew 6:12 AMP

This phrase is the only part of the Lord's Prayer that Jesus continued to teach further about after He gave the disciples the prayer. That tells us that it is very important and we would do well to consider it carefully.

If you are not walking in forgiveness toward others when you pray this, you are actually asking God to be unforgiving toward you. I'm sure that is not what you really desire! It would be better not to pray this phrase at all unless you have forgiven and released all who have hurt you in any way.

In Volume I of my devotional books, I have several days of teaching on forgiveness which you may want to read again if forgiving others is difficult for you.

Forgiveness is an act of your will. If you pray and ask God to flow His unconditional forgiveness through you to the people you need to forgive, He will.

Confess: **"As an act of my will I forgive and**

release_____. I hold no resentment or blame against them."

It may take a while for you to renew your mind and let God change your emotions and feelings toward someone who has wronged you. Just continue to say you have forgiven them and your feelings will be changed.

Prayer: The Lord's Prayer

Today's Scripture Reading: Matt. 18:21-35

Week 18 Day 5
Overcoming Temptation

And lead (bring) us not into temptation, but deliver us from the evil one. Matthew 6:13a AMP

I believe the first part of this verse is requesting help from God to meet the everyday trials of life, and even the heavy troubles that come our way, without being tempted to doubt God's love and care.

James 1:12, 13 says, *"Blessed is the man who perseveres under trial, because when he has stood the test, he will receive the crown of life that God has promised to those who love him. When tempted, no one should say, God is tempting me. For God cannot be tempted by evil, nor does he tempt anyone."*

Verse 12 tells us that we are blessed when we are patient under trial and stand up under temptation. I have been through enough temptations and trials to know that it is often difficult not to be discouraged and get upset at God for "allowing" my problems. But the more I study the Word, the more I realize our problems are a result of our ignorance and/or negative words coupled with the work of the devil as he seeks to destroy us.

61

A pastor I know puts it this way: "The Lord is always voting for us. The devil is always voting against us. We are the ones who cast the deciding vote!"

If we speak negative words that don't agree with God's Word, we are agreeing with satan and he uses this against us.

If we speak words that are in agreement with scripture and also quote exact scriptures, we are agreeing with God. He is then able to work in our behalf and deliver us from the evil one!

Prayer: The Lord's Prayer

Today's Scripture Reading: James 1:12-27

Week 18 Day 6
Our Part in the Kingdom

For Yours is the kingdom and the power and the glory forever. Amen. Matthew 6:13b AMP

Psalm 103:19 says, *"The Lord has established his throne in heaven, and his kingdom rules over all."* Many Christians talk about the sovereignty of God with sort of a "what will be, will be" attitude. "After all," they say, "God is all-powerful and He is in control of everything."

Matthew 19:26 says, *"...with God all things are possible."* This is true, but what God desires to do here on earth is blocked many times by what we say and do.

God's will was for Jesus to heal and perform miracles. Yet Mark 6:5 & 6 says, *"He (Jesus) could not do any miracles there, except lay his hands on a few sick people and heal them. And he was amazed at their lack of faith."* This verse is proof that men's attitudes can actually influence and hinder what God desires to do.

I believe for God's kingdom and power to be revealed so that He receives glory, we Christians need to understand and use the authority God has assigned to us. In Luke 17:21 Jesus said, *"...the kingdom of God is within you."*

Romans 8:19 says, *"The creation waits in eager expectation for the sons of God to be revealed,"* and further in verse 21, *"That the creation itself will be liberated from its bondage to decay and brought into the glorious freedom of the children of God."* (For further insights into this I recommend Agnes Sanford's book, *Creation Waits*.)*

Prayer: The Lord's Prayer

Today's Scripture Reading: Romans 8

*Logos International, Plainfield, NJ 07060 (no copyright date given).

Week 18 Day 7
Let it be Done

Let all the people say, "Amen!" Psalm 106:48

For many years in my Christian life, I didn't know, or even really wonder, what the word "amen" meant. To me it was just a word that signified the ending of a prayer. Then in reading one of Agnes Sanford's books, I discovered her explanation that saying "amen" was like saying, "let it be so" or "it shall be so."

In Webster's dictionary (the reprinted 1828 edition) the definition for "amen" is very interesting and reads, in part: "As a verb, it signifies to confirm, establish, verify. ...In English...it is used...more generally at the end of declarations and prayers, in the sense of: Be it firm, be it established. ...The word is used also as a noun. 'All the promises of God are <u>amen</u> in Christ.' That is firmness, stability, constancy."

You can see it is very fitting and appropriate to end

the Lord's Prayer and other prayers we pray with "Amen."

It is interesting to note that even words we might use as mere ritual such as "amen" have deep meaning and significance.

The Bible is truly a book that one can study a lifetime and never exhaust its depth, wisdom and meaning!

Prayer: The Lord's Prayer

Today's Scripture Reading: II Cor. 1:3-24

Week 19
Communion with God

Week 19 Day 1
Receiving Communion

And day after day they regularly assembled...and in their homes they broke bread [including the Lord's Supper]. Acts 2:46a AMP

In the churches I attended about nine years ago, communion was a quarterly event, the explanation being, if communion was received more often it might become commonplace and meaningless. Then we started attending a church where communion was served every Sunday. I found that taking communion more often had greater, not less, meaning to me. Then I found out that Smith Wigglesworth, a great and powerful man of God, took communion daily and I decided to do the same.

Serving yourself communion may be a new idea to you. Maybe you've been taught that only an ordained minister or an elder or priest can serve communion. I've found nothing in the Bible that says that is necessary. Besides, doesn't Revelation 5:10 say we are priests?

It is important for our spiritual growth to pray, read and study the Bible every day. In the same way, the daily receiving of communion can bless our lives.

Communion should not be taken casually, but with deep reverence and recognition of the tremendous sacrifice made by our Lord and Saviour, Jesus Christ. When taken in this way, I believe it will be a great help to you in your Christian walk.*

Prayer: "Jesus, You made such an awesome sacrifice for me that I cannot even comprehend

65

it. The significance of Your broken body and shed blood is literally beyond knowing. But I do ask that, as much as is humanly possible, I begin to comprehend what You've done for me and that it would change me and help me become more faithful to You.

"Amen."

Today's Scripture Reading: Matt. 26:26-30; Luke 22:14-20

*I suggest that you take communion each day this week as you read the seven devotionals. If it is very meaningful and uplifting to you, you can continue; if not, you need not be "bound" to it and can discontinue it. If you do decide to take communion daily or often, just be sure it does not become a mere ritual to you but is meaningful each and every time.

Week 19 Day 2
Receiving the Bread

While they were eating, Jesus took bread, gave thanks and broke it, and gave it to his disciples, saying, "Take and eat; this is my body." Matthew 26:26

Man is a three-part being; spirit, mind and body (the Bible often says heart, soul and flesh). God is interested in all three parts. The spirit is the most important, of course, because it is the part that lives forever. Also, God wants our bodies whole and pure before Him because they are the temple of His Holy Spirit (I Cor. 6:19, 20).

I believe that the physical suffering Christ went through before and during the crucifixion was for our physical healing.

He was beaten (flogged) by command of Pilate (Matt. 27:26). I Peter 2:24 says, *"By His wounds you have been*

66

healed." Matthew 8:17 says, *"He took up our infirmities and carried our diseases."*

As I eat the bread at communion, I receive it for the healing of my body. I desire that the healing power of Jesus enter and go through my entire being. I thank God for Jesus. Then I thank Jesus for being willing to go through so much physical suffering that I might be healed. I confess that I recognize His sacrifice and receive the benefits into my body.

Prayer: "Jesus, I thank and praise You that You were willing to suffer in Your body that I might have healing for mine. I recognize that sacrifice and receive my healing now. I humbly praise and thank You, Jesus.
"Amen."

Today's Scripture Reading: Is. 53:4-7; Matt. 8:1-17 (Amplified Bible if possible)

Week 19 Day 3
Receiving the Cup

Then he took the cup, gave thanks and offered it to them, saying, "Drink from it, all of you. This is my blood of the covenant, which is poured out for many for the forgiveness of sins." Matthew 26:27-28

The blood of Jesus is an awesome thing. Certainly I do not know or understand the enormity of what the shedding of that blood on Calvary did for me and for all who avail themselves of its cleansing power!

The blood of Christ has so much power in it that when we repent and ask forgiveness for our sins, they are taken wholly, completely and entirely away. In God's eyes it is as though we have never sinned. However, there may still be consequences left over from the sins we've committed, but from God's viewpoint there is no remembrance of the sins. Isaiah 43:25 says God removes them and they are forgotten by Him.

Taking daily communion with the proper attitude and knowledge is a great way of keeping the books balanced each day. Just before you drink the juice, ask God's forgiveness for any sins you've committed and also forgive anyone who has sinned against you. This will keep the record clear between yourself and God, and between yourself and others.

Prayer: "Father God, I do not drink this fruit of the vine lightly or without serious consideration as it represents Jesus' blood. Please help me comprehend the significance of His blood and His sacrifice in my own life. May I always strive to be worthy to receive this gift of God.

"In Jesus' Name, Amen."

Today's Scripture Reading: Romans 5:6-20

Week 19 Day 4
Receiving Worthily

Therefore, whoever eats the bread or drinks the cup of the Lord in an unworthy manner will be guilty of sinning against the body and blood of the Lord. A man ought to examine himself before he eats of the bread and drinks of the cup. For anyone who eats and drinks without recognizing the body of the Lord eats and drinks judgment on himself. I Corinthians 11:27-29

One needs to take communion with a prayerful attitude, recognizing the true significance of it. The body and blood of Jesus are very precious, and one should not partake of them without serious and careful consideration of their meaning.

When I take communion privately I kneel down and humble myself before God. I start with praise and worship to Jesus. Sometimes I use the first part of the 103rd Psalm, but usually I go through the Lord's Prayer as I take communion and personalize it for my own use.

"My Father..." At this point in the prayer I recognize and worship God the Father.

"Thy kingdom come..." I use this as a time to pray God's will be done in my life. I pray for the peace of Jerusalem and for the Jewish people. I repent for our nation's sins and pray for spiritual renewal in America. I pray for our President.

"Give me today my daily bread..." I recognize the bread as representing the body of Jesus and I receive it into myself for healing and strength.

"Forgive me my debts..." I take time to be sure I am walking in forgiveness and love toward all. I recognize the juice as representing the blood of Jesus and I drink it knowing that in His blood is my redemption and forgiveness of sins.

"Lead me not into temptation..." This is a good time to cast down any tendency to sin in your life and ask God to establish a godly trait in its place. An example would be: **"Lord, please deliver me from anger and establish self-control, patience and peace in my life."**

"For Thine is the Kingdom..." This is a good time to again worship and praise God.

Prayer: The Lord's Prayer. Use it as a "springboard" to pray the way I've suggested and personalize it for yourself.

Today's Scripture Reading: I Cor. 11:23-34

69

Week 19 Day 5
Effective Prayer

Do not be anxious about anything, but in everything, by prayer and petition, with thanksgiving, present your requests to God. Philippians 4:6

The attitude you have when you pray is very important. As you pray, your faith should build and peace should come into your heart and mind (Phil. 4:7). Here is a way to pray that will accomplish this.

First, be thankful as you pray. Give God praise and thanks for all the prayers He has already answered. Thank Him for who He is, that you are His child, and for the good things in your life. This will help you lay aside anxiety and fear and build your confidence in Him.

I want you to notice especially the phrase, "...*present your requests to God.*" It does not say -- as people have so often said, "Give all your problems to God!" I believe a "request" is telling God what you need or desire, not a rehashing of your problem.

Pray the <u>answer</u> and not the problem. A negative, complaining and problem-oriented prayer lacks power and does not build your faith. Instead of focusing on the Word and the answer, a negative prayer causes you to focus on the troubles you are experiencing. A positive, solution-oriented prayer will allow hope to enter your heart and will open the door for God to work in your behalf. Here is an example to illustrate what I mean.

Negative prayer: "Dear Lord, please help_____. She has cancer. She is in such terrible pain. Her family is so worried and upset. Please help them, etc."

Positive prayer: "Father God, I lift up _____ today. I ask that the healing light of Jesus go into her body and destroy all cancer cells. I speak life and health to her whole being. I pray that her family will look to You in faith and be encouraged. Bless _____ and her

70

family with strong faith for her healing.
"In the powerful name of Jesus, Amen."

I know you can see the difference in those two prayers and I hope you can feel the difference, too.

Prayer: "Father God, teach me to pray effective and faith-filled prayers that build faith and give hope. Help me pray prayers You can act upon because they present the answers I need to see, rather than the problems that bog me down. Please give me wisdom to pray correctly for each situation that I present to You.
"In Your Son's Name, Amen."

Today's Scripture Reading: Phil. 4:4-8

Affirmation: "I know how to pray powerful, effective, and faith-building prayers. I enjoy my prayer time with God."

Affirmation Scriptures: Ps. 5:3; John 15:7, 16:23, 24; Phil. 4:4-8; Col. 4:2; Heb. 4:16; James 5:16.

Week 19 Day 6
Effective Prayer (Continued)

If you remain in me and my words remain in you, ask whatever you wish, and it will be given you. John 15:7

God doesn't answer just every prayer that is "sent up" to Him. There are some "rules" to be followed if we are to see the answers we desire.
Some people see only the part of the verse that says, *"...whatever you wish will be given you."* Then they are upset when their "wishes" are not granted.

The important requirements to our prayers being answered are that we abide in God and His words abide in us. When we abide in God and His words are a part of our very being, then our wishes (or desires) are in agreement with His will. Then He can and He will answer our prayers.

Matthew 21:22 says, *"If you believe, you will receive whatever you ask for in prayer."* The key phrase here is *"...if you believe."* It is impossible to believe as you should if you don't know whether or not you are praying in agreement with God's will! It is almost impossible to know what God's will is if you do not know what His Word says regarding your prayer request.

You can establish His will in your spirit, heart and mind through research of, meditation on and memorization of God's Word. Then you will be able to pray with faith, truly believing.

Prayer: **"Lord, I have prayed many ineffective prayers because I was not grounded in Your Word and Your ways. I do not want to pray any more "if it be Your will" prayers. Please help me establish what Your will is, through the study of Your Word and the guidance of Your Holy Spirit, so I will know how to pray in agreement with You.**
"In Jesus' Name, Amen."

Today's Scripture Reading: James 1:5-27

Week 19 Day 7
Praying the Word and in the Spirit

The earnest (heartfelt, continued) prayer of a righteous man makes tremendous power available -- dynamic in its working." James 5:16b AMP

There are two ways of praying that I want to present to you today. I believe these ways are powerful and effective.

The first way to pray is to "pray the Word." Quote scriptures as you pray that apply to your prayer requests.

Here are some examples: **"Father, please bless _____ with health. I thank You that by Christ's stripes she is healed (I Pet. 2:24)."** Or, **"Bless _____ with wisdom. Thank You that he has the mind of Christ (I Cor. 2:16) and Jesus is made unto him wisdom (I Cor. 1:30)."** Or, **"Lord, I need special strength today. I thank You that the joy of the Lord is my strength (Neh. 8:10) and that as my day so shall be strength be (Deut. 33:25)."**

There are almost always specific scriptures available in God's Word that we can use to apply to our situations as we pray about them.

The other way to pray, knowing absolutely you are praying in accordance with God's will, is to pray in your God-given prayer language or tongues. Praying in tongues or praying in the Spirit is really the Holy Spirit praying through your human spirit. Since the Holy Spirit is a part of God, you can be sure He would never pray anything that isn't God's will.

I believe the "prayer language" of the Holy Spirit differs from the "gift of tongues" spoken out in some public church services.

I believe that when people receive the Holy Spirit into their hearts (called the filling or the baptism of the Spirit) they have the heavenly language hidden away in their spirits but never use it. This happens because of ignorance, fear, wrong teaching and/or mental blocks.

It is not unusual for Spirit-filled Christians to come to Derin or myself and wonder if they are really Spirit-filled because they haven't as yet spoken in tongues. Often we can "see with our spiritual eyes" the beautiful language that is down in their spirits, just waiting to flow out. When we pray and Jesus sets them free of whatever is blocking the flow, they soon begin to pray in tongues.

It is very sad that there has been so much ignorance, wrong teaching and fear about this beautiful gift of the Spirit when it allows us to pray in perfect harmony with God's will! I hope today's devotional has shed some new light on this subject for you.*

Prayer: "Father, please help me lay aside all false teaching, preconceived ideas, and fear about praying in tongues. I open myself to the complete filling and baptism of Your Holy Spirit. I ask that You would give me every good and perfect gift, including the ability to memorize and pray Your Word and to pray in the language of Your Holy Spirit with freedom and effectiveness.

"As I read today's scriptures, please enlighten my spiritual eyes and reveal the truth to my mind.

"In the Name of the One Who is the Way and the Truth, Jesus, Amen."

Today's Scripture Reading: Rom. 8:27; Eph. 6:18; II Cor. 14:2, 4, 5, 14, 15, 18-21; Jude 20. (Please be aware that in II Cor. 14 Paul is teaching part of the time about tongues spoken in private (the above verses) and other verses are about tongues spoken in public. It is very important to be aware of this distinction. When you are, it can clear up many of the confusing teachings you've perhaps heard in the past on this subject.)

*For further teaching concerning the gifts of the Holy Spirit, see *Image to Image,* Volume I, Week 4.

Week 20
Acquiring Knowledge

Week 20 Day 1
Ignorance of the Word

...my people are destroyed from lack of knowledge. Because you have rejected knowledge, I also reject you as my priests; because you have ignored the law of your God, I also will ignore your children. Hosea 4:6

What knowledge did God's people lack? According to what the verse says, they had rejected knowledge by ignoring God's law, His Word. Many of the Christians today are still ignoring God's Word and because of it are being destroyed spiritually, emotionally, physically, mentally and financially.

The next time a Christian complains to you about illness, mental distress, or financial problems, ask him to quote to you at least three verses from the Bible that give answers concerning God's ways in his area of need. He will be a rare Christian indeed if he can do that for you! No wonder he is getting shot down by satan. He is missing several pieces of his armour as listed in Ephesians 6:14-18:

Belt:	*Of Truth*	*(v. 14)*
Breastplate:	*Of Righteousness*	*(v. 14)*
Shoes:	*Of Peace*	*(v. 15)*
Shield:	*Of Faith*	*(v. 16)*
Helmet:	*Of Salvation*	*(v. 17)*
Sword:	*Of the Spirit --*	*(v. 17)*
	which is the Word of God	

All of the pieces of the *"armour of God"* are linked directly to the Word of God.

No wonder the Word-less, knowledge-lacking Christians are being destroyed! You can change however, and if you have been using this devotional book correctly, you have already been changing. This week will further instruct you, showing you how to acquire knowledge so you will not be destroyed by satan.

Prayer: **"Lord I desire to walk so strongly in knowledge and wisdom that satan cannot ever destroy me, the people, or the things that are precious to me.**

"Guide me into all truth and establish that truth in my mind. Help me be established in Your Word.

"In Jesus' Name, Amen."

Today's Scripture Reading: Prov. 1:29-2:11

Week 20 Day 2
Establishing Knowledge

Teach me knowledge and good judgment, for I believe in Your commands. Psalm 119:66

God desires that we have knowledge of His commands and His ways. That is not possible unless we know what the Bible says.

Joshua 1:8 says to study and meditate in the Word day and night. When we memorize and speak the Word, using it as an integral part of our lives, we can expect God's wisdom and knowledge to become a part of our innermost being (our spirit and heart). It is possible in this way to get the truth of God so established in your heart and mind so that the Word will automatically come to your defense when satan tries to discourage you!

76

A few weeks ago I was under a mental attack from the devil. Almost without thinking, the scriptures that I had memorized and said kept coming to my defense. In a couple of days the battle was over and I was the victor. Don't play "mind games" with satan. Defeat him by doing what Jesus did in Matt. 4:1-11. When He was tempted, He quoted the Word! You can defeat satan in that same way!

Prayer: **"Dear Lord, I need knowledge and good judgment in my personal life and in my relationships with others, especially in my own family. I desire that truth be established in my innermost being (my spirit and heart) and my mind. Help me to meditate in Your Word and use it daily.**
"In Jesus' Name, Amen."

Today's Scripture Reading: Prov. 4:10-27

Affirmation: **"I have knowledge and wisdom because God's Word and ways are established in my life."**
Affirmation Scriptures: Ps. 119, 105; Prov. 1:7, 2:6, 22:17-19.

Week 20 Day 3
Knowledge of God's Ways

For I can testify about them that they are zealous for God, but their zeal is not based on knowledge. Since they did not know the righteousness that comes from God and sought to establish their own, they did not submit to God's righteousness. Romans 10:2, 3

This verse points out the danger of being "turned on" to God without being knowledgeable in His ways.

Many churches have strict rules and regulations for the outward behavior of their members such as no smoking, drinking, dancing, etc. What they have <u>not</u> done is teach their members true knowledge of God's ways so that the inner man could be controlled by the Spirit resulting in no hatred, strife, gossip, condemnation, sin, guilt, or fear.

Too often the fruit of the Spirit (love, joy, peace, patience, kindness, goodness, faithfulness, gentleness and self-control - Gal. 5:22, 23) is not evident in the lives of Christians.

You don't have to spend a very long time witnessing to non-Christians to find out the things that have caused them to see Christians as hypocrites. Non-Christians see some Christians as hypocrites, not because they may smoke, drink, dance or go to movies, but because some Christians are angry and vindictive instead of patient and kind, or dishonest instead of trustworthy.

Our lack of knowledge doesn't just destroy us. It gives satan ammunition to use in destroying others!

Prayer: "Dear Lord, help me to have true knowledge leading to the righteousness of God being established in my life. May my zeal for You be founded in wisdom, with Your fruit evident in my life.

"In Jesus' Name, Amen."
Today's Scripture Reading: Eph. 1 (AMP)

Week 20 Day 4
Our Responsibility

For His divine power has bestowed upon us all things that [are requisite and suited] to life and godliness through the (full, personal) knowledge of Him who called us by and to his own glory and excellence (virtue). II Peter 1:3 AMP

God has called us to excellence. When we have full and personal knowledge of Him, His power enables us to live godly lives. This verse expresses the opposite of Hosea 4:6 which says that we perish, or are destroyed, because of our lack of knowledge.

People put much responsibility on God by saying He causes or allows illness (or other problems) in the lives of Christians. The truth of the matter is that many Christians lack knowledge of their authority through the blood of Jesus, the empowering of the Holy Spirit and the correct knowledge and use of the Word. This allows satan to put sickness and problems on them!

This authority is not taught from most pulpits. However, it is taught in the Bible and I believe God is going to hold us responsible as to whether or not we read His Word and use it in our lives!

Prayer: "Dear Lord, may the eyes of my heart be enlightened as I read Your Word so that I acquire true knowledge of Your ways. Help me to apply this knowledge in my everyday life so that I reflect Your glory and excellence in my own home and to the hurting world.
"In Jesus' Name, Amen."

Today's Scripture Reading: II Peter 1 (Note especially verse 2, Amplified Bible)

Week 20 Day 5
Having Wisdom

[For I always pray] the God of our Lord Jesus Christ,...that He might grant you a spirit of wisdom and revelation -- of insight into mysteries and secrets -- in the [deep and intimate] knowledge of Him. Ephesians 1:17 AMP

To me, wisdom is knowing how to correctly use the knowledge I have already. There are churches and organizations that emphasize the memorization of Bible verses, and that is good. However, along with memorization of scripture, churches need to teach people how to apply what they have memorized, by practical application and revelation, in their everyday lives.

Personally, I have been helped by putting the verses I've memorized into categories such as faith, hope, self-control, peace, etc. In this way, I have been able to memorize and remember verses better. I know better which verse or verses I need to quote when I'm doing battle against the devil. For instance, when battling against fear it is much more helpful for me to quote II Timothy 1:7 (AMP) which says, *"For God did not give us a spirit of ...fear -- but [He has given us a spirit] of power and of love and of calm and well-balanced mind and discipline and self-control,"* rather than Colossians 3:13 which says, *"Bear with each other and forgive whatever grievance you may have..."* I like to be specific in my battle against satan, using the weapon that is appropriate for the battle.

The Word was given to us for use daily so we can be more than conquerors in Christ Jesus. James 1:22 says that He who is wise will be a doer of the Word, not just a hearer.

Prayer: "Lord, teach me how to apply my knowledge of Your Word so that I have wisdom in my life. Through the power of Your Holy Spirit, please guide me into the revelation of the truth that is in the Bible. I ask that You establish wisdom in all areas of my life. Help me to know the correct use and application of Your Word.

"In Jesus' Name, Amen."

Today's Scripture Reading: Prov. 8:1-21

Week 20 Day 6
The Blessings of Wisdom

Blessed is the man who finds wisdom, the man who gains understanding. Proverbs 3:13

The book of Proverbs has much to say about wisdom. There are many benefits and blessings that are attained by the person who has wisdom.

Several of these benefits are mentioned in this third chapter as: Favor and a good name with God and man (v. 4); health in your body (v. 8); long life and riches (v. 16); and protection and safety (v. 23).

In recent years health and prosperity have become favorite sermon topics for many of the "Word" preachers.

Some people have thrown away their medicine and glasses and started confessing for health. Others "claimed" money, cars, planes and big houses. They were confused and angry with God when they didn't receive what they had confessed. I believe these people were not taught how to use wisdom. We have been taught that Psalm 37:4 says, *"...he will give you the desires of your heart."* But included in this verse is the condition to, *"Delight yourself in the Lord."*

Some people are in danger of making material things their delight, because they haven't been taught to distinguish between a desire of the heart and the wants of the mind or fleshly desires.

True wisdom will teach us the difference. King Solomon asked for wisdom first. Then he received the riches we so often hear about.

Proverbs 8:18 (AMP) in speaking of wisdom says, *"Riches and honor are with me, enduring wealth, and righteousness [that is, uprightness in every area and relation, and right standing with God]."* One of the verses given as a cross reference is Matt. 6:33 (AMP). It says, *"But seek for (aim at and strive after) first of all His kingdom, and His righteousness [His way of doing and being right], and then all these things taken together will be given you besides."*

Prayer: "Lord, teach me to distinguish between the true riches You would give to me and the materialism my flesh desires.

"Please give me wisdom to discern between true and false riches. Help me to put Your kingdom first in my life and to walk in wisdom so that I am in a position spiritually to be trusted with prosperity and riches.

"In Jesus Name, Amen."

Today's Scripture Reading: Prov. 3

Week 20 Day 7
Acting in Wisdom

Who is wise and understanding among you? Let him show it by his good life, by deeds done in the humility that comes from wisdom.

...the wisdom that comes from heaven is first of all pure, then peace loving, considerate, submissive, full of mercy and good fruit... James 3:13 & 17

So many times the Bible talks about the fruit in people's lives. We charismatics need to be careful that we don't get caught up in the gifts of the Holy Spirit and neglect to walk in wisdom, cultivating the fruit of the Spirit in our lives. We need to remember that the Bible teaches we can know a person by his fruit, but nowhere does it say that we are known by the gifts.

The gifts of the Holy Spirit (see I Cor. 12, 14)) are good. I would not want to be without them, but we shouldn't get so involved in them that we neglect the fruit of the Holy Spirit (see Galatians 5:22, 23). Our style of living, our way of life, and our deeds should reflect the qualities of Jesus.

Proverbs 11:30 says, *"The fruit of the righteous is a tree of life, and he who wins souls is wise."* I think it could also be said that he who is wise, wins souls. The world is desperately looking for answers. Christians who know the Word and walk in God's wisdom can give answers to people who are seeking, and thus be able to lead many to Jesus.

Prayer: "Father, in my relationships to others, I desire to walk in wisdom and mercy. May they see the fruit of Your Spirit in my life and because of that, be drawn to You.
"In Jesus' Name, Amen."

Today's Scripture Reading: Prov. 1:26-2:11

Week 21
Overcoming Anger

Week 21 Day 1
Overcoming Bitterness

...Let every man be quick to hear (a ready listener), slow to speak, slow to take offense and to get angry. For man's anger does not promote the righteousness God [wishes and requires]. James 1:19, 20 AMP

Anger and its companions (unforgiveness, resentment and bitterness, which lead to malice and hatred) is probably the area where the "world" most often criticizes "Christians." People who are not born again feel that we as Christians are hypocrites because of the anger and hostility they feel directed toward them, and many times this is so evident, even to our fellow Christians. If we Christians would only get this one important area under God's control, our impact on the world would be greatly enhanced (to say nothing of the peace, harmony and joy that would be added to us and to our homes)!

If you are a person who is easily prone to anger, this week's devotion can literally change your life. I plead with you to take the prayers, affirmation and scriptures and apply them diligently to your life, letting God give you the self-control and inner peace you so desperately need.

Prayer: "Lord, I repent of the sins of unforgiveness, anger, hostility, bitterness and hatred in my life. I turn away from them and I ask that You would replace them with a forgiving attitude, self-control, love and a peaceful spirit.

"Forgive me for all my sins caused by anger

and remove the spirit of bitterness from my life. Help me to diligently renew my mind so I will be able to walk in love and forgiveness as You did here on earth.

"In Jesus' Name, Amen."

Today's Scripture Reading: James 1:12-27

Affirmation: "**My emotions are controlled by the Holy Spirit. I am peaceful, self-controlled and kind.**"

Affirmation Scriptures: Prov. 14:29, 17:27b, 29:11, 22; Eccl. 7:9; Eph. 4:26, 27; I Thes. 5:14 (AV).

Week 21 Day 2
Forgiving

Be kind and compassionate to one another, forgiving each other, just as in Christ, God forgave you. Ephesians 4:32

The first step to getting rid of anger in your life is to forgive. I have found you can forgive people as an act of your will whether you <u>feel</u> like it or not.

You achieve this forgiving attitude by saying: "**As an act of my will I choose to forgive and release _____. Lord, please forgive me for being angry at _____ and flow Your forgiveness through me to him/her.**"

Since you choose to forgive, you have forgiven. If satan still tempts you to be angry, hold a grudge or desire to "get even" with that person, remind him that you have forgiven and that your attitude about others is now in God's control. Start thanking God that He is helping you walk in love and forgiveness toward all people.

Do you remember when Peter asked Jesus in Matt.

86

18:21, 22, how many times he should forgive a brother who sinned against him? Jesus replied, *"Seventy times seven."* I really think He meant to forgive as many times as necessary and don't keep count.

I know it is difficult to forgive someone who repeatedly hurts you. However, as you walk in forgiveness and pray for that person, it opens a powerful channel for God to work through to change that person -- especially if the one you are forgiving is your spouse!

Prayer: "Father, forgive me for walking in anger and bitterness in the past. I now choose to walk in forgiveness and love. Help me to always be quick to forgive.

"In the Name of Jesus, Who forgave me of all my sins, Amen."

Today's Scripture Reading: Matt. 18:21-35

Don't forget to say aloud your affirmation and scriptures on forgiveness! (See *Image to Image,* Volume I, Week 3 Day 3, or use our ministry's *Scripture Cards,* specifically the scriptures on forgiveness.)

Week 21 Day 3
Forgive Quickly

"In your anger do not sin:" Do not let the sun go down while you are still angry, and do not give the devil a foothold. Ephesians 4:26, 27

I think there are times when even Spirit-filled Christians get angry. This verse tells us not to let that anger turn into a sin by harboring it and letting it last over night.

Balance the books each day by letting forgiveness flow and letting God take your anger away. This is especially important in marriage and family relationships. Don't go to bed angry at your spouse or children. If you do, satan can gain a foothold of bitterness. Unforgiveness leading into bitterness can "poison" the whole atmosphere of your home.

In the past, when anger was strong in my life, Derin says that when he would walk through the door of our house he could feel that I was upset and angry. Now, people comment that our house is so "homey" and peaceful. The anger and strife are gone and are replaced with the love and harmony of the Spirit of God.

Our family has learned to ask God's and each other's forgiveness for being angry. We use God's Word in our home to help us live peacefully with each other. I praise God for showing us how to walk in His ways!

Prayer: "Lord, please help me not to harbor anger or resentment in my heart. Help me to be quick to forgive and walk in peace and love, especially in my own home, and with those I love, my family.
"In Jesus' Name, Amen."

Today's Scripture Reading: Ps. 101:1-3; Eph. 4:17-6:4

Week 21 Day 4
Overcoming Anger with Wisdom

A fool gives full vent to his anger, but a wise man keeps himself under control. Proverbs 29:11

As shown in the book of Proverbs, the control of one's anger is linked with understanding and wisdom (Prov. 14:29, 17:27). Other verses in Proverbs urge us to seek wisdom and understanding. Proverbs 8:18 tells us that wisdom brings riches and honor.

Our ministry once received a letter from an angry man. He began the letter by reprimanding us and ended his letter asking questions as to why God wasn't prospering his family's finances. I felt led by the Holy Spirit to write that man and tell him that his angry attitude was blocking God's ability to bless and prosper him. I was somewhat hesitant to send the letter (as the things that I said were blunt) and I didn't want to make the man even more angry. But, praise God, the Holy Spirit had prepared his heart and we soon received a letter back thanking us for telling him the truth.

He asked our forgiveness and told us he had forgiven us and the others with whom he was angry, so that now the channels to God's blessings in his life were open.

I admire people who are open to new light from God! I believe there is always room for growth and new revelation in our Christian walk. Don't let the traditional teachings and doctrines of your church keep you from receiving new insights from the truth of God's Word!

Prayer: "Dear Lord, I ask that the eyes of my heart be enlightened to any hidden anger in my life.

"Lord, for too long satan has deceived me, causing me to call the sin of anger "righteous indignation". I ask that my wrong attitudes be forgiven and taken from me. Please replace them with self-control, kindness and patience.

"In Jesus' Name, Amen."

Today's Scripture Reading: Prov. 14:17; 15:1

Week 21 Day 5
Overcoming Anger with Love

A gentle answer turns away wrath, but a harsh word stirs up anger. Proverbs 15:1

This verse is especially important to practice in your home. If you are accustomed to meeting your child's or spouse's anger with yelling and harsh words, memorize and start practicing this verse.

It is amazing how reasonable words said in a calm and quiet voice can help a person gain self-control again. There are even times when the Lord tells me just to be quiet and say nothing at all.

I'm not referring to the "silent treatment" given out of anger. I am referring to a stillness that fosters peace and harmony between you and your child or mate. This is what Ephesians 6:4 says in the Amplified Bible: *"Fathers, do not irritate and provoke your children to anger -- do not exasperate them to resentment -- but rear them [tenderly] in the training and discipline, and counsel and admonition of the Lord."*

Angry and unreasonable parents raise angry, rebellious children. Parents who have God's Word memorized and established in their spirits, so they are controlled by it, can raise children who are cooperative, obedient and strong in the Lord.

What is your choice?

Prayer: **"Dear Father, Your Word teaches me what kind of parent I should (and can) be. Help me to put away all anger, grudges and malice. Help me to walk in forgiveness and love toward my family. May they see the loving attitude of Jesus in my life.**
"In His Name, Amen."

Today's Scripture Reading: Phil. 4:5-9; Col. 3:12-21 (Amplified Bible if possible)

Week 21 Day 6
Overcoming Anger with the Fruit of the Spirit

Be eagerly seeking after peace with all...exercising oversight (over yourselves) lest anyone be falling away from the grace of God, lest any root of bitterness springing up be troubling you, and through this the many be defiled,... Hebrews 12:14, 15 WUEST

Many people live in bitterness. They often blame God for the things in their lives that brought pain and anger. John 10:10 says that Jesus came to give us abundant life and James 1:17 says that God is the giver of every good and perfect gift. These verses are not real to their hearts or established in their minds. Because of this, they blame God for things that satan has done to them and have become double-minded. James 1:6-8 says that a double-minded man cannot receive anything from the Lord. Consequently, God cannot answer their prayers.

Such people are usually angry with other people in their lives, too, such as their parents, employer and/or spouse. Because they are not walking in forgiveness, there is a blockage of God's blessings to them (see Matthew 6:15).

If you are a bitter person, not only will bitterness cause grave problems in your life, but it will carry over into the lives of people around you, especially your husband or wife and your children. However, if you will repent and pray, your bitterness can be replaced with a peaceful, joyful, forgiving, and loving attitude.

Prayer: "Father God, I admit I have been bitter and angry toward You and others for the hurts and frustrations of my life. I ask Your forgiveness for this and I ask that Your forgiveness will flow through me as I release all those to whom I have been angry to You.

"Please take away all bitterness, and replace it with unconditional love. Help me to daily walk in love toward You, others and also

91

myself.
"In Jesus' Name, Amen."

Today's Scripture Reading: Heb. 12:14; 13:8

Week 21 Day 7
Spiritual Exercise

...Train yourself toward godliness...keeping yourself spiritually fit. For physical training is of some value...but godliness [spiritual training] is useful and of value in everything and in every way, for it holds promise for the present life and also for the life which is to come.
I Timothy 4:7, 8 AMP

Physical fitness has become almost a fixation for many people. Books on exercise, jogging, etc. have become best sellers. I agree that it is important to keep physically fit, but it is much more important to be spiritually fit.

Athletes are in training for physical endurance. Christians need to be in training for spiritual endurance and godliness.

The benefits of being spiritually fit for this life are wonderful. Since eliminating (almost all) anger from my life, I am happier, healthier and have a peace I didn't before possess.

If you will examine your anger (of the past, I hope), you will find that many times the cause was selfishness. Usually people are angry when "self" is inconvenienced or doesn't get its way. If you will let God have what you consider are "your rights", much of your cause of anger will be gone. The heart of a true servant of God is seldom angry or resentful.

Prayer: **"Father, help me to have an**

unselfish, patient, and kind attitude of service to others. I yield all my rights to You. Please take away all selfishness and strife from my life. "In Jesus' Name, Amen."

Today's Scripture Reading: Phil. 4:5-9; Col. 3:12-21
(Amplified Bible if possible)

Week 22
Overcoming Pride

Week 22 Day 1
Being Humble-Minded

...God sets Himself against the proud and haughty, but gives grace (continually) to the lowly -- those who are humble-minded enough to receive it. James 4:5 AMP

Self sufficiency is a form of pride. People who feel they can make it on their own without God are operating in pride.

Have you ever felt as if God Himself was against you? Then you need to examine your attitudes and see if you are walking in pride, because this verse says, *"God sets Himself against the proud."*

Because we Christians have satan and his demons always against us, we especially need to be sure we are humble before God so that He is able to be <u>for us!</u>

In Mark 10:24, Jesus talks about the difficulty a rich man has getting into His kingdom. The reason could very well be that those who are wealthy tend to look at their wealth and think, "Look what I have accomplished! <u>My</u> hard work and bright mind have given me great success. Why do I need God?" Proud people do not stop to realize that without God's blessings of health, strength and a good mind, they would be unable to do the things they accomplish. They say, "I am a self-made success," instead of giving God the glory and praise He deserves.

Prayer: "Dear Lord, please reveal to me any pride that is in my life. I want You to take out all pride of self and self-success.

95

"Lord, I ask that You put an accurate understanding of myself and of You into my heart and mind. Help me to walk in humility and honesty before You.
"In Jesus' Name, Amen."

Today's Scripture Reading: James 4 (in Amplified Bible, if possible)

Week 22 Day 2
Developing Humility

...get rid of all...wickedness, and in a humble (gentle, modest) spirit receive and welcome the Word which implanted and rooted [in your hearts] contains the power to save your souls. James 1:21 AMP

Pride is one sin which is very skilled in defending itself. Ego does not want to give up the rule in our lives and is pleased to keep us deceived in this area of our hearts.

We need to be aware that pride can take many forms. I really think that being negative about yourself is a form of pride. Some people are proud of their humility! Putting yourself down, having a poor self-concept, is not true humility. I believe true humility is the ability to see yourself as God sees you and to accept that true and right picture of yourself.

Today's verse says that we are to receive the Word with a humble spirit. The Word has much to say about who we are as Christians. Accepting what the Word says about us and living in harmony and agreement with it leads to true humility. God's Word will open up the door for God's blessings in your life!

In this week's devotionals I will endeavor to show you the way to a truly humble and gentle spirit which will bring God's grace and favor into your life.

Prayer: "Lord, I want to see myself accurately. I want to know how You see me and to know who I am in Christ Jesus.

"Lord, please remove all the blockages from my past and help me to have a heart that is open to Your Truth.

"In the Name of the Truth Giver, Jesus, Amen."

Today's Scripture Reading: Proverbs 15:33-16:25

Week 22 Day 3
A Servant's Heart

Whoever exalts himself [with haughtiness and empty pride] shall be humbled...and whoever humbles himself -- who has a modest opinion of himself and behaves accordingly -- shall be raised to honor. Matthew 23:12 AMP

When you get rid of pride and begin to walk in humility, rewards start coming your way. Proverbs 29:23 says, *"...a man of lowly spirit gains honor."*

People do not want to give honor to someone who demands it, or who they feel is egotistical. But a person who has a humble attitude naturally draws the favor of people to himself.

We had the pleasure of meeting Pat Boone in 1983. He has been famous and well-known for years and would have, in man's way of thinking, reason to be proud. But instead he was very humble, polite and kind, not acting as if he was better than we in any way. I believe he truly has a servant's heart. Since then, when someone talks to me about Pat Boone, I am quick to "honor" him by giving a good report on what a neat person he is and that I feel he is a sincere and true Christian.

I wish that Pat's sweet attitude would be typical of all well-known Christians! There would be fewer accusations from the world that Christians are hypocrites.

If pride has been a problem for you, today's affirmation will help you develop an attitude of true humility.

Prayer: "Dear Heavenly Father, I want the right attitude and evaluation of myself. Help me to see myself as You see me and make any changes that I need to make in order to have true humility and a servant's heart.
"In Jesus' Name, Amen."

Today's Scripture Reading: Proverbs 18:6-15

Affirmation: "I have the humility of Jesus in me. I know how to serve others. My attitude is like Christ's."

Affirmation Scriptures: Dan. 4:37; Prov. 16:5, 18, 18:12, 29:23; Matt. 5:5; Mark 10:43; Luke 12:15, 14:11; Eph. 4:23; Phil. 2:5.

Week 22 Day 4
The Humility of Jesus

...and those who walk in pride He is able to abase and humble. Daniel 4:37 AMP
Pride goes before destruction, a haughty spirit before a fall. Proverbs 16:18

It is much better to take the Word and discipline ourselves to get rid of pride and wrong attitudes, as an act of the will, than to have to be disciplined and brought down through God's chastisement. It is even worse to be disciplined by the destruction satan is able to bring against us through the open door of pride.

So I encourage you to use yesterday's affirmation,

even if you don't feel pride has been a problem in your life. It certainly won't hurt you to confess for a servant's heart and that the attitude of Jesus is within you!

Jesus served willingly and gave of Himself to beggars, lepers, tax collectors, the sick and the demon possessed. On the other hand, Jesus was tough on the religious leaders who were proud of their traditions and religious practices. Jesus could do all of this with confidence and self-control because He knew who He was in His relationship to God, His Father.

To have the humility and effectiveness of Christ, we must understand and accept our place as God's children and His place as our Father. God's desire is that we would possess true humility by seeing ourselves as He sees us and having the knowledge of who we are in Him.

Prayer: "Lord, I desire to have an accurate view of myself, one in agreement and harmony with Your Truth. Thank You for helping me overcome pride. Now, help me to establish in my heart and mind a correct self-concept based on Your Word.

"In Jesus' Name, Amen."

Today's Scripture Reading: James 1:5-27 (in Amplified Bible). *Note especially verses 9 and 21.*

Week 22 Day 5
Confessing Sin

The Lord does not look at the things men look at. Man looks at the outward appearance, but the Lord looks at the heart. I Samuel 16:7b

It is interesting to me that even people whom I consider to be committing serious sins write our ministry saying, "More than anything else I want to serve God."

Many of you reading this today have an area in your life where you yield to satan's temptation again and again. It may be as "small" a sin as an occasional day of depression and self-pity or as "large" a sin as lust and adultery.

Whatever the sin is, it opens the door for satan to accuse and condemn you and keeps your life from being as effective for God as you desire it to be. God does not want you in bondage to any kind of sin!

The Bible contains many verses about peace and freedom. Romans 8:6 and John 8:32 are two of my favorites: *"...The mind controlled by the Spirit is life and peace ."* and *"...You will know the truth, and the truth will set you free."*

But, if you are not free and don't have inner peace, the Word says you can have it. It is a matter of:

(1) Repenting of the sin.

(2) Asking God to establish the opposite godly trait in you. For example, ask for purity instead of lust, peace and joy instead of depression, etc.

(3) Receiving by faith what the Word says, believing (agreeing with God's view as found in His Word) and then confessing it, that you have what you've asked of God.

(4) Refusing to give in to satan's lie that you haven't really received by standing firm on your confession!

Prayer: "Lord, I repent of _____ and ask Your forgiveness. I confess release from its bondage.

"I ask You, Lord, to establish _____ in its place. Thank You for giving me _____.

"I will walk in _____ from this day on. I resist the devil and say he must flee from me (James 4:7).

"I confess I am forgiven and free in Christ.

"In His precious Name, Amen."

Today's Scripture Reading: John 8:2-11, 31-58

Week 22 Day 6
Overcoming Satan

It is for freedom that Christ has set us free. Stand firm, then, and do not let yourselves be burdened again by a yoke of slavery. Galatians 5:1

We often hear about people's free will. One of our main beliefs is that God will not violate our will and I believe that is true.

However, I think there are some who have forgotten that satan has no such rule in his dealings with us. Satan loves to get you to do things against your will.

Again, we get letters saying, "I want to do God's will. I want to be a good Christian, but I cannot break the habit of _____," and they name the sin that has them in slavery.

Drug addicts, alcoholics, homosexuals, and even smokers are desperate for help. They want to be free from their bondage, but are held captive by satan against their free will! They need help from a friend or relative to come against satan and bind him, giving them an option of choosing God and His ways.

If you are in bondage to some deception of satan, ask a strong Christian friend or relative to agree with you that the bondage will be broken. Then your mind and body will be free to agree with your spirit so you can do God's will in your life.

Prayer: "Lord, I want to be free in You. I come against satan and his strongholds in my life and I say he cannot hold me against my will. I will to will the will of God. I choose to walk in God's ways.

"Thank You, Lord, for giving me the strength to step into Your kingdom of light and true freedom.

"In the Son's Name, Amen."

Today's Scripture Reading: Gal. 5:13- 6:10.

Week 22 Day 7
God's View of You

If anyone thinks he is something when he is nothing, he deceives himself. Each one should test his own actions. Then he can take pride in himself, without comparing himself to somebody else. Galatians 6:3, 4

Don't measure who you are by man's standards. Check your actions by the measure of God's Word. Then you can have a self-concept that is correct.

Luke 6:43-45 says we will know God's people by their fruit. Galatians 5:22, 23 list the fruit of the Spirit as love, joy, peace, patience, kindness, goodness, faithfulness, gentleness and self- control. These should be evident first at home, to your own family, and then to others around you.

Another fruit God desires you to produce is the salvation of people to whom you witness. If your actions are not producing fruit, you need to seek God until you find out why.

Ask God to show you yourself as He sees you. Listen to His still small voice. Look in His Word.

There is a fine balance here between pride, correct self-esteem, and true humility. God wants you to have a true and right balance and when you are sincere in seeking it, He will lead you into that balance. It is what I call congruence -- harmony of spirit, heart, mind and body. It is what I continually desire to achieve.

Prayer: "Lord, I desire to be whole and harmonious in spirit, heart, mind and body. I open all of myself up to You and ask that Your

Holy Spirit go through every part of my being and my life. Reveal any areas where I need to change.

"Lord, help me to walk in the light You bring, and into fullness of confidence, peace, freedom and joy.

"In Jesus' Name, Amen."

Today's Scripture Reading: Psalm 119:30-48

Week 23
Becoming Congruent

Week 23 Day 1
Being Whole

And may the God of peace Himself sanctify you through and through -- that is separate you from profane things, make you pure and wholly consecrated to God -- and may your spirit, soul and body be preserved sound and complete [and found] blameless at the coming of our Lord Jesus Christ, the Messiah. I Thessalonians 5:23 AMP

The word "congruent" may be one you haven't heard used very often, so I will give you the definition of it from Webster's dictionary (1828 edition): Congruent: Agreeing. Congruity: The relationship of agreement between things; consistency.

My desire is that we Christians become free, whole and congruent, submitted to and directed by God's Holy Spirit, having our spirit, heart, mind and body in tune with Him. In Mark 12:30, Jesus talked about loving God with all your heart, soul, mind and strength. God was interested in man's wholeness long before our modern day doctors and psychiatrists got the idea.

It is interesting to see how much man has studied and developed ways to treat physical and mental illnesses, but how little is known about spiritual health. Even churches and Christian schools have failed to teach about the importance of man's spirit and heart. Your spirit is the part of you that is immortal and will live forever. Your heart contains the *"issues of life"* and is to be kept with diligence (Prov. 4:23).

Achieving wholeness will take consistent meditation in the Word along with fasting and prayer. It is not an easy task, but it is worth doing to become free and whole!

Prayer: "Lord, I want to be free from any sinful bondages in my life that are affecting my spirit, heart, mind or body. I pray You would give me the spiritual strength and mental self-discipline to walk in Your ways and achieve wholeness and harmony in my life. "In Jesus' Name, Amen."

Today's Scripture Reading: I Peter 1:13-2:12.

Week 23 Day 2
Inner Freedom

Behold, You desire truth in the inner being; make me therefore to know wisdom in my inmost heart... Create in me a clean heart, O God; and renew a right, persevering and steadfast spirit within me. Psalm 51:6, 10 AMP

The most important part of you is your spirit and heart. To become what God desires you to be, you must open up your heart to receive Christ as your Saviour. Then you must yield to the Holy Spirit, letting His power come in to cleanse, sanctify and establish your heart in righteousness.

When you receive Christ, according to II Cor. 5:17, you become a new creation. You are given a new heart within. You are reconciled to God and your sins are forgiven and forgotten. They are forgotten by God, but often you remember your sins all too well. Because it is not easy to forget your sin, you do not receive fully the reality of God's love and forgiveness.

Many people are still troubled in their spirits and minds by the sins they've committed and those sins that

106

were committed against them. Also, the natural consequences of these sins still affect them. They need special healing of their spirits and hearts before they can sense that they are truly free in the Lord. (See Chapter Four of my book, *Set My Heart Free,* or Week One of *Image to Image,* Volume I, for further teaching in this area.)

Today's prayer will open the door to that healing.

Prayer: "Father God, I ask for and receive Jesus Christ and the Holy Spirit into my heart. I ask that all the sins and hurts of my past be forgiven and healed. As an act of my will I forgive all who have sinned against me or hurt me in any way.

"I ask You, Father, to remove all bitterness, anger, fear and guilt from me. I yield them all up to You and I receive Your healing light into my spirit and heart. I ask that Your light remove all darkness from me.

"In Jesus' (Who is pure Light) Name, Amen."

Today's Scripture Reading: Ps. 51:1-17

Week 23 Day 3
Renewed Mind

[For being as he is], a man of two minds -- hesitating, dubious, irresolute -- [he is] unstable and unreliable and uncertain about everything (he thinks, feels, decides). James 1:8 AMP

In this verse we have a picture of a man who is double-minded. His spirit, heart and mind are not in alignment. He may have a new heart because of what God has done for him spiritually, but his mind still contains the old thought patterns that have been there since childhood.

Satan is very determined to keep those thought patterns that way, too! He wants you to keep your false guilt and your fears since they are not in agreement with your spirit now that it has been born-anew into God's kingdom.

You will notice, as you read today's scriptures, that a double-minded person doesn't receive answers from the Lord (v. 7). If you are a double-minded person, the doubts in your mind conflict with the faith in your heart, and those doubts and fears block God's power from working in your life. This can be overcome by the renewing of your mind. In the New English version, Romans 12:2 says, *"Let your minds be remade and your whole nature thus transformed."*

When your *"whole nature"* is transformed, you will become what your heart has desired you to be for so long -- a person who is in harmony with God and with your own self, whole and congruent in spirit, heart, mind and body. This did not happen, for me, overnight. I had to memorize and use scriptures to renew my mind over a period of time.* But, praise God, my mind is now trained to think as His Word says I should and I know how to bring my thoughts into harmony with my spirit!

Prayer: "Lord, I desire that my mind be harmonious with my new heart. I desire to be single-minded in Your ways. Help me to have the self-discipline to memorize Your Word and use it daily in my life.
"In Jesus' Name, Amen."

Today's Scripture Reading: James 1:5-8, 16-27

*(For an affirmation and scripture concerning a renewed mind, see *Image to Image,* Volume I. Page 29)

Week 23 Day 4
Being Single-Minded

Teach me your way, O Lord, and I will walk in your truth; give me an undivided heart... Psalm 86:11

In his book, *I Will Lift Up Mine Eyes,** Glenn Clark tells a story about riding a horse that was not sure-footed enough to be ridden on a narrow mountain trail.

Mr. Clark explains about *"hind's feet"* (as used in Psalm 18:33 - KJV), relating it to our being single-minded so we can climb to the *"high places"* that God has for us.

This book by Glenn Clark was the one that started me into a new and deeper walk with the Lord about 13 years ago and literally changed my life.

A phrase we often hear today is that someone needs to "get it together" and how true it is of many people. I don't know of any way we can get ourselves together without God and His Word and the help of the Holy Spirit!

Instead of "getting it together," the world seems to be falling apart, going more and more into fear, confusion, division, divorce and broken family relationships, and chaos.

Your life can be an oasis of peace, order, togetherness and harmony through the yielding of yourself wholly to the Holy Spirit, releasing all bitterness of the past and becoming saturated in God's Word.

You must become as James 1:22 says, " ... a *doer of the Word."* That is a person who uses the Word daily to overcome temptations, doubts or false thinking, and all of the lies from the devil.

I have found the best way to resist the devil and make him flee is to use the Word by quoting it to him. He doesn't like to hear the Word and he will leave. Sometimes it takes several scriptures before he is

*Harper and Row, New York and Evanston

convinced that you are not going to "buy his lies", but he can be convinced!

Prayer: "Lord, I want to be single-minded and have singleness of purpose in my life. Help me to establish the Word in my spirit, heart and mind so satan cannot deceive me in any way. Thank You for wholeness and harmony in my life.
"In Jesus' Name, Amen."

Today's Scripture Reading: James 4:1-10 (Amplified Bible, if possible)

Affirmation: "I have singleness of purpose to serve God with my entire spirit, heart, mind and body. I am single-minded about the truth of God's Word."

Affirmation Scriptures: Ps. 86:11; Matt. 6:33; II Tim. 1:12b; Heb. 10:23; James 1:5-8

Week 23 Day 5
Setting Your Mind

For those who are according to the flesh and controlled by its unholy desires, set their minds on and pursue those things which gratify the flesh. But those who are according to the Spirit and [controlled by the desires] of the Spirit, set their minds on and seek those things which gratify the (Holy) Spirit. Romans 8:5 AMP

We get letters from Christians crying out for help because they are continuing to sin in their flesh, but their spirits are desiring to live a holy life before God. They say things like this: "I want to do God's will. I want to live

110

close to God, but I can't stop_____!" Some have even said they would rather be dead than continue in the sins they abhor!

What has happened to these people is that their desires and the lusts of the flesh are controlling their minds. Instead of letting their minds be controlled by the flesh, they must learn how to let the Holy Spirit control their minds.

Our mind is the battle ground for satan, and he uses our fleshly desires, presenting evil imaginations, doubts and fears. He provides "reasons" for bitterness and anger, lust, greed and pride, not to mention many other things.

God, through His Word and the gentle Holy Spirit, presents thoughts that are holy, faith-filled, confident, forgiving, loving, pure, generous, humble, etc.

If we let our flesh control our minds, we will be caught in the web of sin and evil desires. If we are controlled by the Holy Spirit, we will be free to walk in God's ways of peace and love.

In the next few days, I will be giving you teaching, that if applied faithfully, will set you free to live by the Spirit and not your flesh.

Prayer: **"Dear Heavenly Father, I know that there are two ways to live. One is the way satan and my flesh, or body, wants to live, and the other is the way Your Word says I should live.**

"As an act of my will, today I choose to give my life over to the control of the Holy Spirit. I desire to have my mind controlled by the Spirit and to think on "whatever is true, ...noble,...right,...pure,...lovely, ...admirable, ...excellent or praiseworthy... (Phil. 4:8).
"In Jesus' Name, Amen."

Today's Scripture Reading: Romans 8:1-18
(Amplified Bible)

111

Week 23 Day 6
Controlling the Flesh

So, since Christ suffered in the flesh [for us, for you], arm yourselves with the same thought and purpose ...For whoever has suffered in the flesh [having the mind of Christ] has done with [intentional] sin -- has stopped pleasing himself and the world, and pleases God. So that he can no longer spend the rest of his natural life living by [his] human appetites and desires , but [he lives] for what God wills. I Peter 4:1, 2 AMP

Some believe the "suffering" written about in this chapter in I Peter means sickness, but it doesn't. If sickness caused people to quit sinning, we would have a lot less sin in this world than we do!

There are many forms of suffering in our flesh that I believe are designed to put down the bodily appetites and desire to sin. Self-discipline is one form of suffering. I will try to explain this through an illustration from my own life.

There are some things I thoroughly enjoy doing--for instance, reading a good book. But since God has placed me in this ministry, I have less and less time for the things that I want to do. I must discipline myself more and more to spend time in prayer, Bible study, writing and ministering to people. I cannot always do what my "flesh" wants to do.

Fasting is another area in which God calls us to "suffer." I have had very few people tell me that fasting was easy for them. For me it takes determination and self-control and I "suffer" as I do it.

Another "suffering" we will have as we grow strong in the Lord and pure in our flesh, is that other people will not understand. Some will be convicted by our lifestyle and will come against what we are doing. We will meet with persecution, often from other Christians, and we will

112

"suffer" because of the hurt of their words and false accusations.

I believe this is the kind of suffering God desires us to be willing to endure for Him. I believe sickness is put on us by satan and that we should resist it! (See Week 14 of this book.)

Prayer: "Lord, I am opening up my life to You. I am willing to suffer to bring my flesh into submission to Your will.

"Lord, help me to cast down fleshly lusts and sins. Help me to live in purity of heart, mind and body.

"In Jesus' Name, Amen."

Today's Scripture Reading: I Peter 4:1-8

Week 23 Day 7
Aligning Spirit, Heart, Mind and Body

Now the mind of the flesh [which is sense and reason without the Holy Spirit] is death -- death that comprises all the miseries arising from sin, both here and hereafter. But the mind of the (Holy) Spirit is life and soul-peace [both now and forever]. Romans 8:6 AMP

In the New International Version of the Bible, the second part of this verse says,"...*the mind controlled by the Spirit is life and peace.*" So many people are seeking to have a fulfilling life and inner peace, but it eludes them because they are controlled by their flesh instead of the Holy Spirit. This is even true of many Christians. I believe God is calling Christians today to purify their hearts and become single-minded, with hearts fully committed to Him and with their minds controlled by His Spirit. When our minds aren't controlled by the Spirit and the Word, our flesh is really in control.

113

This leads to spiritual death and often physical death, also. We are seeing the results of flesh oriented living all around us. These results are selfishness, manipulation, lust and sexual sins, greed, divorce, drug abuse, and suicide. Society continues to seek cures for these problems through education, social programs, mental health clinics, etc. These programs may help to a certain degree, but they cannot make the real changes in lives that are needed.

But God's Spirit can help us become singleminded! As we Christians yield ourselves totally -- spirit, mind and body to God, and truly give our hearts to Him, we will see changes in ourselves, our families, our churches, in our society and our nation.

Prayer: "Lord, our world needs to be changed. Please begin with me by giving me a heart that hungers for righteousness.

"Lord, give me a mind that casts down vain imaginations and is saturated in Your Word.

"I ask You, Jesus, to give me a body that is disciplined and controlled by Your Holy Spirit within me.

"In Jesus' Name, Amen."

Today's Scripture Reading: Romans 8 (Amplified Bible, if possible)

Week 24
Establishing Righteousness

Week 24 Day 1
How About Your Heart?

For the eyes of the Lord range throughout the earth to strengthen those whose hearts are fully committed to him.
II Chronicles 16:9

For a long time I thought the Bible used "heart" when it meant "spirit." I found out this is not the case. Knowing what the Biblical term "heart" means has caused new enlightenment to come into my life. I would like to share some of these truths with you.

(I must give credit where credit is due and say the reason I've gotten hold of this "new truth" is because of the teaching on the heart presented by our pastor, John Stocker.)

In checking the Hebrew and Greek meanings, I found "heart" meant the innermost part of man, the seat of his emotions and his will. The "spirit" of man is the immortal part of him that lives eternally.

According to scripture we can have a hardened heart (Eph. 4:18), a deceitful heart (Jer. 17:9), a wicked, unbelieving heart (Heb. 3:12), etc.

When we come to Christ, He puts a new heart within us but we must be careful that we don't let our hearts slip back into old habit patterns of feeling and become corrupted again.

If satan can get us to doubt God's ways and His love, we can develop hearts that harbor unbelief and hearts that lose the fervent love we had for God when we first came to Him and were born again.

We are to watch over our hearts with all diligence

115

(Prov. 4:23). We need to understand that we cannot be passive. We need to know the Word and use it -- being doers of the Word (James 1:22-25).

We also need to have the fruit and gifts of the Holy Spirit within, giving us power to overcome the devil and his demons and revealing God's Truth to us.

Prayer: "Dear Lord, I desire to have a heart that is open to You, a pliable heart that You can mold, a heart of flesh that has sensitivity to the voice of Your Holy Spirit. Open up the eyes of my heart as I study this week, so that I will have understanding of why it is so important that my heart is fully committed to You.

"In the Name of Christ Jesus, Amen."

Today's Scripture Reading: II Chron. 16:7-17:6
See *Zech. 7:8-14* on hardened hearts.

Week 24 Day 2
A Yearning Heart

But (Jehoshaphat) *sought and yearned with all of his desire for the Lord the God of his father and walked in His commandments, and not after the ways of Israel. II Chronicles 17:4 AMP*

In yesterday's scripture reading (II Chron. 16:7-17:6) you clearly see the contrast between two men; one who didn't listen to God or walk in His ways and one who did.

Asa, (who didn't follow God) got a disease which became very severe and he died.

Jehoshaphat followed God, and his kingdom was established, he had great riches and honor, his heart was cheered and his courage was high. (Amplified Bible)

116

Even though God's ways haven't changed, since Jesus came and the Holy Spirit was given, it has become easier to know God's will and be empowered to walk in it.

Today those who fully follow God are blessed. The United States and Switzerland both speak of God in their founding papers. These nations are blessed and prosperous.

Haiti was dedicated to satan when it was founded as a nation. As a result, there is great proverty and oppression in Haiti. The contrast is obvious!

Recently I talked with a man who was angry at God because of the suffering and sin in our world. He was blaming God for what we, in our ignorance and unbelief, have allowed satan to do in our world. (See Week Seven on *Establishing Righteousness* in *Image to Image,* Volume I.)

Sometimes it is easier and more comfortable to point our finger at God and cry, "Why?" than it is to take a close look at our own heart and life and see if we are living a life that God can justifiably bless.

We keep looking for God's mercy (and He has an abundance of that, praise His Name!) when we need to be studying and learning what the Word says about the "ground rules" for receiving His blessings!

Prayer: "Heavenly Father, I praise You for Your mercy, but I want to go further in a mature walk with You and come to a deep knowledge of Your Word, Your ways and Your Truth.

"Holy Spirit, You were sent to reveal Truth to me. I open the eyes of my heart to see and know that Truth.

"In Jesus' Name, Amen."

Today's Scripture Reading: Jer. 4:10-22, 5:1-31, 7:23 (Amplified Bible, if possible)

Week 24 Day 3
A Repentant Heart

And the Lord your God will circumcise your heart, and the heart of your descendants, to love the Lord your God with all your [mind and] heart, and with all your being, that you may live. Deuteronomy 30:6 AMP

In Mark 12:29, 30 when Jesus was asked about the most important commandment, He replied, *"Love the Lord your God with all your heart...soul...mind and...strength."*

It is impossible to love God with all of your heart when any of it is in rebellion to Him. Whatever is in your heart that is not of God (unforgiveness, anger, bitterness, pride, jealousy, lust, coveteousness, greed, unconfessed sins, even fear) will block the free flow of love and devotion to God. Anything not of God will block His ability to give you the full blessing He desires you to have in your life.

II Cor. 7:9-11 speaks of a godly sorrow that leads to repentance. In the Old Testament, God often called His people to repent, to turn away from sin and to seek Him with their whole hearts through messages from the prophets. In Joel 2:13, He tells them to rend their hearts instead of tearing their clothing.

In counseling a man who had been in an adulterous relationship for about 20 years, I found he had words in defense of his sin. A spirit of deceit and lust held him captive. I told him to pray that God would show him how He viewed his sin and that God would give him sorrow that would lead to repentance.

You may be thinking, "How could someone be involved in an affair and not feel guilty?" The answer is that he had a hardened heart. Years of telling the voice of the Holy Spirit, his conscience, to be quiet as he justified his actions, had caused his heart to callous over so he did not feel a need to repent.

118

Before you become too judgmental toward this "Christian" man (who, by the way, had been active in his church many years) examine your own heart. Make sure there is no sinful attitude such as anger or pride that you may have had for so long that you are no longer "bothered" with feelings of sorrow or guilt about it.

"Prayer: "Lord, show me what is truly in my heart. I ask you to circumcise my heart and cut away any hard callouses that prevent me from hearing Your still small voice and thus be led to godly sorrow and repentance. I pray that You would give me godly sorrow right now over any sin that is within me and I now determine to turn away from it and walk in Your ways!
"In the Name of Jesus, my Saviour, Amen."

Today's Scripture Reading: II Cor. 3:12-18; James 4:8-10

Week 24 Day 4
A Calloused Heart

For the heart -- the understanding, the soul -- of this people has grown dull (stupid, hardened and calloused) and their ears are heavy and hard of hearing, and they have shut tight their eyes, so that they may not perceive and have knowledge and become acquainted with their eyes, and hear with their ears, and understand with their souls, and turn (to Me, be converted) so that I may heal them. Acts 28:27 AMP

In this verse Paul was teaching Jews who weren't willing to accept the gospel, and he was quoting what the prophet Isaiah had said to the Jews centuries before (Isaiah 6:10).

119

In Isaiah's time, and throughout the Old Testament, God strove to reveal Himself to the Israelites as their loving heavenly Father. Even though they saw His mighty miracles and heard many truths (and warnings) from the prophets, their hearts were still hardened. They refused to come to an understanding of God as their Father.

Then Jesus came. His life fulfilled perfectly what was prophesied in the Old Testament. He was the Son of God, their Messiah. He performed many miracles, including raising the dead.

Jesus taught with a great authority, so they marvelled at His great wisdom. Yet they did not receive Him. They persecuted and reviled Him and at last crucified Him on Calvary.

In the book of Acts the Holy Spirit was given to the earth. He is a fulfillment of what Jesus said would happen after His death and resurrection. After receiving the baptism of the Holy Spirit, the disciples performed many miracles and prophesied. They taught with authority and knowledge. Again, the Jews hardened their hearts and rejected God's Spirit. They stoned, imprisoned and killed His apostles.

Today God is still striving to reveal Himself to the Jews, the Gentiles, and to all people everywhere. Supernatural miracles are still happening. Prophesies are given and the Word of God is being taught with power and authority.

Yet many are arguing over theological differences and holding to traditional teachings of denominations (the doctrines of man). Their hearts are hardened, full of unbelief as they again persecute those who walk in the ways of the Holy Spirit. In Genesis 6:3 God says, *"My Spirit will not always strive with man."*

Through these thousands of years, God in His mercy has been endeavoring to reveal Himself to mankind. Many people, both Jew and Gentile, rejected Him as their loving Father. They rejected His only Son. They are still rejecting His precious Holy Spirit. It is amazing that He is still lovingly calling people to Himself. He is truly a merciful and long suffering God!

Prayer: "Lord, I open up my heart. I acknowledge that You are my Father. I confess Jesus is Your Son and I accept His sacrificial death for the forgiveness of my sins. I open my spirit and heart to receive Your Holy Spirit and His fruit and gifts in my life.

"I pray that people everywhere, especially those who are Christians, will be open to the Holy Spirit and all that You have through Him for them.

"May we all be enlightened to the truth of Your Word and empowered to walk in love and authority as Jesus did.

"In the Name of Jesus, Your Son, Amen."

Today's Scripture Reading: Acts 28:16-31

Week 24 Day 5
The Believing Heart

...*"The word is near you; it is in your mouth and in your heart,"...That if you confess with your mouth 'Jesus is Lord,' and believe in your heart that God raised him from the dead, you will be saved. For it is with your heart you believe and are justified, and it is with your mouth that you confess and are saved. Romans 10:8-10*

Sometimes, as I write these devotionals, I feel as though I am almost too "heavy" while trying to teach and inspire people to walk closer to God. My goal, as I write, is to help people change so they are in a better position to receive God's blessings in their lives.

I do not want to criticize or condemn. I want to say, "Let me show you a better, more excellent way."

I am so encouraged to see God's people who are walking in righteousness to the very best of their abilities! On our T.V. program, when our pastor taught on fasting, I was encouraged when many of our listeners wrote in asking for the tapes. People who are dedicated enough to fast, are desiring to see God work in their hearts.

This matter of serving the Lord with all your heart, mind and strength is not easy. It will take prayer, fasting, and concentrated study of the Word. But the joy and blessings He gives, as we give Him our whole hearts, are worth it all.

Maybe you are saying, "I want to give God my whole heart. I want to have a heart that is always open to Him, but I am not sure how to do it." As in so many areas, the confession of our mouth is the key. Ask for, receive, believe and confess that you have a heart that is open to God and you will have it.

Prayer: **"Lord, I ask that You cleanse my heart from all unrighteousness and unbelief. Make it open to You. Thank You for taking away my heart of stone and putting a heart of flesh within me (Ez. 11:19). I believe I have received it.**
"In Jesus' Name, Amen."

Today's Scripture Reading: Romans 10:6-17

Affirmation: **"My heart is open before God. I will serve Him with my whole heart. The Holy Spirit is making my heart perfect toward God."**

Affirmation Scriptures: Ps. 51:6, 10, 17; I John 2:5

Week 24 Day 6
A Wise Heart

Behold, You desire truth in the inner being; make me therefore to know wisdom in my inmost heart.   Psalm 51:6 AMP

After King David was rebuked for his sin by Nathan, the prophet, he did what I directed you to do in yesterday's devotions. He asked God to cleanse his heart, to renew his spirit and to restore joy to him.

As you read this 51st Psalm, you will find that David had a godly sorrow that led to a prayer of sincere repentance. And God heard and answered that prayer and the fellowship between David and God was restored.

The sins of adultery and murder which David committed were very serious. Certainly, the just nature of God could never condone them. Yet, in Acts 13:22, God says that David was, *"A man after My own heart."* How can this be? It is because of God's loving mercy and because David had a truly repentant heart. He turned from his sin and began to walk in obedience to God. God recognized that his repentance was genuine and even though this happened before Christ's atonement on the cross, David was forgiven and given a pure heart in God's sight.

How much more, since atonement by Jesus has been made, are we able to receive forgiveness and be given a new heart when we are open and honest before God?! So, in faith, continue to confess the affirmation I gave you yesterday, allowing God's Spirit to work in your heart.

Prayer: **"I thank You, Father, that You have forgiven my sins and cleansed my heart by the blood of Jesus. I will do my part to keep my heart open to Your Spirit and clean through the washing of the Word (Eph. 5:26).**
"In the Name of Christ, Amen."

123

Week 24 Day 7
A Perfect Heart

May the Lord make your love increase and overflow for each other and for everyone else, just as ours does for you. May he strengthen your hearts so that you will be blameless and holy in the presence of our God and Father when our Lord Jesus comes... I Thessalonians 3:12, 13

Above all else, guard your heart, for it is the well-spring of life. Proverbs 4:23

In Matthew 5:48 Jesus instructs us, *"Be perfect, therefore, as your heavenly Father is perfect."*

You may feel that being perfect is an impossibility. I know it is not an easy command to follow. But if it weren't possible, I don't think Jesus would tell us to do it .

To attain the perfection God tells us to have, we will have to watch over our hearts with all diligence (Prov. 4:23). We also have to walk in God-given love toward all, including our enemies.

You do not need to talk very long to people, Christian or non-Christian, before you hear them say that some Christian person has cheated them, lied to them, gossiped about them, etc. In fact, many businessmen will tell you they would rather do business with worldly people than Christians.

Recently, we needed something done for our ministry. A "Christian brother" said he would do it for $2,000. A non-Christian man said he would do it for $2.00! One might wonder if the Christian, who was going to charge $2,000 for the same task, was acting in love.

A perfect heart will eliminate dishonesty and cheating of others. It will rid the churches of strife and unforgiveness. Anger, bitterness and selfishness will go. And the world will see in us trustworthiness, honesty and integrity. They will know us by our love (John 13:34, 35).

The world will see in us the fruit of the Holy Spirit as listed in Gal. 5:22 & 23: *"...love, joy, peace, patience, kindness, goodness, faithfulness, gentleness and self-control ."*

"And so faith, hope, love abide;...these three, but the greatest of these is love (I Cor. 13:13 AMP)."

Love makes perfect!

Prayer: **"Dear loving Father, my desire is to have a perfect heart, but I know I cannot do it on my own. I must look to Your Word, walk consistently in Your ways and be led and empowered by Your Holy Spirit.**

"This day I set my will to walk in forgiveness and love as You have commanded.

"Lord, please help me to live up to this choice.

"In the strong Name of Jesus, Amen."

Today's Scripture Reading: Hebrews 3:7-15, 4:11-16, 8:10, 11

Week 25
Fasting

Week 25 Day 1
Why Fast?

But the time will come when the bridegroom will be taken from them, and on that day they will fast. Mark 2:20

The people were asking Jesus why His disciples were not fasting and the above verse is His answer. There are many places in the Bible where fasting is mentioned but I have heard very few sermons about it!

I was probably in my 30's before I heard a teaching on fasting at the Bill Gothard seminar. At that time I started fasting, but I really didn't have any spiritual insights on why I was doing it. I was not always as consistent in fasting as I should have been.

Also there were times when I fasted because I was upset and I was going to "force God" to do something. Let me tell you, with that kind of attitude, fasting doesn't work! You can fast until you die and God won't be "forced" into helping you. Out of His mercy and loving-kindness He might come to your aid -- but it is much better to know the principles and reasons for fasting so it will be effective in your life and on behalf of others.

This week I will endeavor to help you see the reasons and the benefits of fasting.

Prayer: "Lord, I am opening my heart to receive Your truth on fasting. As light about fasting is shed on my heart, please help me to walk in that light and make fasting a regular part

of my life.
"In Jesus' Name, Amen."

Today's Scripture Reading: Isaiah 58:1-12

Week 25 Day 2
Fasting to Establish Self-Control

...you shouldn't be so concerned about perishable things like food. No, spend your energy seeking the eternal life that I, the Messiah, can give you. John 6:27 LB

It seems as though the people in the United States have a fixation on eating! Far too many of us eat a lot more than we need. That is why such a high percentage of people are overweight. Last fall we were in Switzerland for about two weeks. It was interesting to note that the people there have a whole different attitude about food than we do. And I saw almost no fat people there!

In Matthew 6:25 Jesus said, *"Life is more important than food."* And in Luke 12:29 He said, *"Do not set your heart on what you will eat or drink."*

But, it is like we have been "programmed" since childhood to give food top priority! It is not easy to undo this fixation on food. Fasting is a good way to let your body know you are going to live according to the dictates of the Spirit -- not your flesh (Romans 8:1 AMP).

When you fast for an entire day (or three meals) you become aware of how your body has had a stronghold in your life in the area of eating. It is amazing how strongly it demands food when not fed every four to six hours!

Fasting, drinking only water for a 24-hour period, shows your flesh you are serious about getting it under the control of the Holy Spirit. It will help you break the habit of overeating! (For more insights on overeating, See *Image to Image,* Volume I, Week 10).

128

Prayer: "Father, my desire is that Your Holy Spirit be in control of my body, especially over my eating habits. "Lord, forgive me for bad eating habits. Please help me order my eating in a new way as You would have me do.

"I ask You to give me strength and determination to fast regularly to establish self-control in my life.

"In Jesus' Name, Amen."

Today's Scripture Reading: Luke 12:13-34

Week 25 Day 3
Fasting for Physical Benefits

Man does not live on bread alone, but on every word that comes from the mouth of God. Matthew 4:4

In our society we have made food and eating far too important. We "train" our children to overeat by making them eat everything on their plates or "just one more bite" when they are already full.

In her book, *The Diet Alternative**, Diane Hampton explains how God gave us natural responses of hungry and full. Because we eat on a schedule instead of when we are hungry and then eat until we are overstuffed, not just full, we have messed up the natural, God-given restraints that would help us be temperate and self-controlled in our eating.

I believe fasting is helpful in breaking the overeating habit. Fasting also has other physical benefits. It helps clear out toxins and poisons that are in our bodies. It helps break the habits of smoking, drinking alcohol and/or drug abuse. It causes us to lose weight.

*Copyright 1984 Whitaker House, Springdale, PA.

Be sure to drink plenty of water while you are fasting. Two quarts a day is what is recommended. (Do not drink soda, coffee or tea during your fast.)

Recently the Lord called me to a three-day fast. It was really a blessing to me. The first two days were somewhat difficult, but by the third day it was easier. Here are some of the benefits I received.

I lost the four to five pounds I'd been trying to lose for several months. I felt really encouraged spiritually because I had been obedient to God. I knew I could control my flesh and say "no" to food over a period of time. I had been able to "...live *not after the dictates of the flesh, but after the dictates of the Spirit (Rom. 8:1 AMP)."*

If you have never fasted for three (or more) days, I suggest you do it. You will see some neat results.

Prayer: "Father, my desire is to be obedient to Your Holy Spirit in all areas of my life. I do not want to be controlled by my fleshly appetite. Please cause my fasting to be of spiritual and physical benefit to me. May my fasting draw me closer to Your perfect plan for my life. "In Jesus' Name, Amen."

Today's Scripture Reading: Matt. 6:25-34

Week 25 Day 4
Cautions About Fasting

So whether you eat or drink or whatever you do, do it all for the glory of God. I Corinthians 10:31

If you have any type of illness, are pregnant or nursing, please check with your doctor before fasting. Also check (even if you are in good health) before going on a fast of longer than seven days.

When you break a fast of more than two days, it

should be done by drinking juice -- don't eat a large meal immediately.

If you are serious about fasting more than a day at a time, I suggest you get a book that gives clear instructions on how to break a fast and what physical symptoms to expect while fasting.

If you are addicted to caffeine, you may have a headache from giving up your coffee, tea or cola. You may feel weak at times.

As your body cleanses itself, you may experience various pains or discomforts. Don't be discouraged or give up -- feed on the Word, pray in the Spirit and give God praise for strength!

I try to choose a day when I can be home and don't have lots of heavy physical work to do. I also try to get some extra rest (like a nap) on the days I fast.

One-day fasts are good for self-discipline, maintaining weight loss, and a spiritual discipline of obedience to God.

Longer fasts are excellent for losing weight, cleansing your body, breaking bad habits, getting rid of fleshly lusts and spending time in intercession and communion with God.

Prayer: **"Lord, please help me to fast in the way You desire. Help me to use fasting as a method to grow and mature in You.**
"In Jesus' Name, Amen."

Today's Scripture Reading: II Chron. 20:3-30

Week 25 Day 5
Correct Fasting

When you fast, do not look somber as the hypocrites do,...but when you fast, put oil on your head and wash your face, so it will not be obvious to men that you are

fasting, but only to your Father, who is unseen; and your Father, who sees what is done in secret, will reward you.
Matthew 6:16-18

Some people seem to think fasting is optional or unnecessary in their Christian walk. Please note that this verse says "when", not "if" you fast. I'm sure you can choose not to fast and still be a Christian and go to heaven. But the benefits from fasting, both spiritual and physical, are so great that I believe every Christian should fast regularly.

The Bible doesn't seem to have rigid rules concerning fasting. Rather, fasting is mentioned as if it is just an assumed practice for God's children. It is mentioned many times in both the Old and New Testaments.

Matthew, Mark and Luke have all recorded that Jesus said His disciples would fast after He was gone away from them. In Acts 13 and 14 you find reports of people in the church fasting and worshipping God. They also fasted before making some important church decisions.

Of course, our most important example of Christian living is Jesus, who fasted for 40 days before beginning His ministry to others. If Jesus, whose relationship to God, His Father, was perfect, needed to fast, certainly we would be very presumptuous to assume that it is not necessary for us to do the same. This is especially true if you intend to have a ministry to others, whether you are a teacher, pastor, evangelist, prophet or apostle.

Prayer: "Lord, I offer my fasting up to You as a sacrifice of obedience. I pray that it will break all bondages in my life that are not in line with Your ways.

"During times of fasting I ask that You circumcise my heart, removing all hardness of heart, making me tender and sensitive to Your Holy Spirit.

132

"I want every yoke of bondage or hindrance to perfect fellowship with You removed, so that I will walk in total obedience to Your Spirit. Help me to establish fasting as a regular habit in my life, to strengthen my spiritual heart and keep my walk with You pure and holy.

"In Jesus' Name, Amen."

Today's Scripture Reading: Matt. 4:1-11

Affirmation: "In obedience to the Lord and His Word, I will fast as a regular weekly discipline and at special times as God leads me."

Affirmation Scriptures: Ezra 8:21-23; Ps. 35:13, 69:10; Is. 58:6; Matt. 6:16-18, 9:14, 15; Acts 13:2, 3.

Week 25 Day 6
Fasting Unto the Lord

Ask all the people of the land and the priests, "When you fasted and mourned in the fifth and seventh months for the past seventy years, was it really for me that you fasted?" Zechariah 7:5

It is of utmost importance that your fast be an act of obedience and sacrifice to God, for spiritual discipline and spiritual growth.

In the past few days I have given you some of the physical and health benefits of fasting, but the benefits that are most important are the ones that will change your heart and make it more open and obedient to God.

Apparently, the people to whom the prophet Zechariah was talking had fasted regularly for 70 years and still hadn't done it for the right reasons. The instructions given to them in chapter 7, verses 9 and 10 were to: *"Adminster true justice; show mercy and compassion* to one another. *Do not oppress the widow or the fatherless, the alien or the poor. In your hearts do not think evil of each other."*

Fasting should soften your heart and give you a desire to walk in God's ways, being obedient to His Word.

Matthew 4 tells us that Jesus fasted 40 days before He began His ministry. I am sure, during that time, He and the Father had a close communion and He was being strengthened for the difficult ministry ahead of Him, including Calvary.

Jesus walked in perfect obedience to God. Just preceding this fast, when Jesus was baptized by John (Matt. 3:17), the voice of God came from heaven saying, *"This is my Son, whom I love; with him I am well pleased."*

After the fast, Jesus was able to resist powerful temptations from the devil, and angels came and attended Him. Then He immediately began His ministry -- preaching, calling His disciples, and healing the sick.

We are to be doing the same things that Jesus did (John 14:12). Perhaps the reason so few of us really do them is because we have not prepared ourselves (denied ourselves) through prayer and fasting unto the Lord.

Prayer: **"Father God, I humble myself before You and ask that You place a desire in my heart to fast. Help the primary goal in my fasting to be obedience to You that *"Your kingdom come, Your will be done on earth as it is in heaven (Matt. 6:10)."***

"In the Name of Jesus, Your obedient Son, Amen."

Today's Scripture Reading: Matt. 3:13-4:25

Week 25 Day 7
Godly Fasting

Is not this the kind of fasting I have chosen; to loose the chains of injustice and untie the cords of the yoke, to set the oppressed free and break every yoke? Isaiah 58:6

The Israelites were complaining to God. They said that God had not seen their fasting or noticed their humility. God said they couldn't expect to be heard by Him because they weren't fasting for the right reasons or in the correct way. I did three days of that kind of fasting a few years ago. Believe me, it was very difficult and the results were nil.

For several years I fasted two or three meals, or one day a week, as a self-discipline. The benefits were very few.

Recently our pastor taught on fasting. I praise the Lord for his obedience and enlightenment. While listening to his teaching my heart and mind were opened to see the real reasons for fasting,* and I was led to do some additional reading and study on my own.** Since then, I have fasted occasional meals, one day a week, and once for a three-day period. I am now fasting with new knowledge for the correct reasons, and I am seeing the benefits, blessings and spiritual growth that result from fasting.

Acts 13:2 (Revised Version) says, *"They ministered to the Lord, and fasted."* Remember Proverbs 3:6 (LB) says, *"In everything you do put God first..."* That includes fasting. When our priorities are right, God can and will bless us. He fulfill His promises to us.

Prayer: "Lord, I desire to minister to and serve You as You direct. I offer myself as a living sacrifice to You (Rom. 12:1). I will deny myself and take up my cross and follow You (Matt. 16:24).

135

"Help me follow the example of Jesus and the Apostle Paul by fasting in obedience and worship to God.

"In Jesus' precious Name, Amen."

Today's Scripture Reading: Isaiah 58

*Tapes of these sermons on fasting are available through *Resurrection Fellowship*, Loveland, Colorado.

**For further study on fasting, I recommend: *God's Chosen Fast* by Arthur Wallis, *Your Appointment With God* by Gwen Shaw, and *Atomic Power with God with Fasting and Prayer* by Rev. Franklin Hall.

Week 26
God's Light

Week 26 Day 1
Christ's Light in You

You are the light of the world...let your light shine before men, that they may see your good deeds and praise your Father in heaven. Matthew 5:14a, 16b

As you walk in purity of heart, in fasting, and in wholeness of spirit, mind and body, you will be a wonderful light in the world.

Several years ago in Glenn Clark's writings I read about being incandescent with God's light. It was something I desired in my life, so I began to pray that God's light would shine in and through me. I prayed this for probably two or three years and really didn't see it happen as I was envisioning it should. Then in April of 1978 I realized I should quit asking and start confessing that Christ's light was in me! I saw an immediate result to this confession. It was as though I had all of a sudden developed a magnetism that attracted people. Apparently their spirits were drawn to the light of Jesus in me. And I learned an important lesson: When you ask for something that you know is His will, especially something spiritual-- after you have asked -- receive it! Don't keep asking over and over for it. Start confessing you have it. Start thanking Him for the answer.

Matt. 7:7 says, *"Ask and you will receive."* Believe it! When we ask a friend for a favor, we believe he/she will do it for us and we usually thank them in advance. Do the same with God's promises!

Prayer: "Dear Father, I thank You that You desire to do good things for me. Help me to

understand Your love for me and know what my inheritance is as Your child.

"Please make me a beacon that shines brightly with Your light in this world. Thank You, Lord. Amen."

Today's Scripture Reading: Matt. 5:13-16

Affirmation: "Christ's light is in, on and around me drawing people to Him."

Affirmation Scriptures: Psalms 34:5, 36:9, 37:6, 118:27; Prov. 4:18, 13:9; Is. 60:1; Dan. 12:3; Matt. 5:14-16, 13:43; John 3:21, 8:12; II Cor. 3:18; Eph. 5:8, 9.

Week 26 Day 2
Confess Light

Those who are wise will shine like the brightness of the heavens, and those who lead many to righteousness, like the stars forever and ever. Daniel 12:3

I want you to try an experiment this week. I challenge you to say the affirmation on light along with scriptures on light every morning for at least a week. Then notice how people react to you.

Recently Derin got a call from a lady who was desiring to be a better witness to people. She said she had never led anyone to receive Christ and she very much wanted to do so.

If you are desiring to be a better witness, confessing God's light is a good place to start. Most people have difficulty going up to complete strangers and asking if they are saved. But, when Jesus' light in you is so bright that people are naturally drawn to you -- and they begin to come to you for help -- it will be much easier to talk to them about their relationship with God.

138

As you confess that Jesus' light is within you drawing people to Him, you will begin to see them being drawn. Be aware, in your conversation with them, of an opening to speak to them of the things of God. Ask the Holy Spirit to guide you in order to witness to them effectively.

Perhaps you won't lead them to accept Christ right then and there, but you can plant the seeds that will bring fruit that you or someone else can harvest later. Just be open to the Spirit's leading and let your light shine!

Prayer: "**Dear Lord, when I get to heaven, I want to bring those I have led to You with me. I want to bring many souls into Your kingdom.**

"**Help the light of Jesus to be so radiant within me that people will be drawn to You through me. Then bless me with wisdom and the courage to share the good news of Your gospel with them.**

"**In the Name of Jesus, the Light-giver, Amen.**"

Today's Scripture Reading: Eph. 5:8-21

Week 26 Day 3
Seeing God's Light

For with you is the fountain of life; in your light we see light. Psalm 36:9

Life and light are from God. Satan's kingdom is the kingdom of darkness. Eph. 5:8 says we were once darkness, but now we are light in the Lord. We have been transferred from the kingdom of darkness into the kingdom of God's dear Son (Col. 1:13) and that kingdom is light! If we will open the eyes of our hearts and let them be enlightened (Eph. 1:18) we will see, or understand this light. There are so many riches in God's Word!

If you will use your concordance and look up all the verses on light, asking God to give you revelation knowledge in this area, I know it will be a blessing to you.

Last spring we met a lawyer who used to be an alcoholic and had a very sinful lifestyle. His conference room was very brightly lit. He told us that before he became a Christian his conference room was kept dimly lit. Now he wanted it light.

John 3:19 says, *"Men love darkness because their deeds are evil."* Isn't it interesting to see that even sinners are living out what the Word says without being aware of it?

It is sad, on the other hand, that many who say they are Christians are not walking in the light as they should. Some are perishing for lack of knowledge (Hosea 4:6) and others have allowed their hearts to become hardened to God's voice. Their light is dim and the world has difficulty seeing God's love in their lives. Determine today not to be that kind of person!

Prayer: "Lord, help me to have a tender and pliable heart toward You. Help me to have wisdom in my walk with You and my relationships to others.

"May I be a pure vessel from which Your light can radiate, illuminating both my mind and life and the lives of those to whom I witness.

"In Jesus' Name, Amen."

Today's Scripture Reading: Eph. 4:17-32

Week 26 Day 4
Keeping Bright

And all of us, as with unveiled face [because we] continue to behold [in the Word of God] as in a mirror the glory of the Lord, are constantly being transfigured into His very own image in ever increasing splendor and from one degree of glory to another; [for this comes] from the Lord [Who is] the Spirit. II Corinthians 3:18 AMP

This verse is the source of the title for my devotional books. I desire so very much that God's children be able to see Him, know Him, understand His Word, and because of that be transfigured into His image! That is the whole purpose of my writing these books. (It is a big job and I'm certainly not doing it just for fun!)

I want us, as Christians, to be so filled with the light of Jesus that others are irresistibly drawn to the light. So many have let their lamps become tarnished! "Small sins" creep into their lives, almost before they know it.

Derin and I are saddened that so many Christians are not totally honest. If it makes things look better for them, they will lie. To make a little more money, they will cheat in a business deal and lie on income tax returns -- after all it is only "the government" that they are cheating!

I was raised by my parents to be totally honest. My conscience absolutely refuses to let me get by with dishonesty! I keep expecting that kind of honesty from other Christians, but I am sorry to say that many of them have lied to us and cheated our ministry. They have not fulfilled promises or kept their word to us. We have, as an act of our will, walked in forgiveness toward them.

I do not believe this is the way it should be. It is very hurtful in our witness to the non-Christians, who, by the way, have often been more fair and honest with us than our "Christian brothers!"

Prayer: "Lord, please give me godly sorrow and a spirit of repentance over any dishonesty in my life. I want to walk totally in truthfulness and fairness so that Your Light in me will not be dimmed by deception of any kind.

141

"Lord, in You there is no shadow of darkness at all -- You are pure Light.

"Please help me to daily live so that your Light is unhampered from shining in and through me, that I may draw people to You.

"In Jesus, the Light-bearer's Name, Amen."

Today's Scripture Reading: II Cor. 3:12-4:7

Week 26 Day 5
Walking in the Light

The path of the righteous is like the first gleam of dawn, shining ever brighter till the full light of day. Proverbs 4:18

We get many letters from Christians who are depressed. Usually their letters are full of negative confessions. They are looking at the circumstances of their lives and seeing defeat and despair.

I know what depression and discouragement are like, because I used to have them. But since I have learned to use the Word every day, I am free from depression. You can be, too.

Get established in righteousness. At first, you may see only a small glimmer of the light of hope and encouragement. But as you persist in walking in the path of righteousness, you will walk into the full light of joy and faith.

As doubt, discouragement, depression and self-pity go, God will be able to shine His full light into your life, giving you the peace and gladness of heart that you need.

It is up to you to start on that path and to walk in it each day until you are in the *"full light of day."* As you begin, you may see only a small amount of light, "the first gleam of dawn," but as you are faithful to do the Word daily, you will see the light increasing until you are free.

Psalm 97:11 says, *"Light is shed upon the righteous and joy on the upright in heart."* Take that verse as your promise from God!

Prayer: "Lord, I repent of bitterness, self-pity and depression. I ask You to remove them from my life. I ask You to replace them with a forgiving attitude and confidence in Your love and the joy of the Lord.

"Give me strength to walk daily in the path of righteousness until I see Your full light and Your gladness in my life.

"In Jesus' Name, Amen."

Today's Scripture Reading: Proverbs 4

Week 26 Day 6
Jesus is Our Light

Arise, shine, for your light has come, and the glory of the Lord rises upon you. Isaiah 60:1

Much of Isaiah is prophecy about Jesus. When Jesus came He said, *"I am the light of the world. Whoever follows me will never walk in darkness, but will have the light of life (John 8:12)."*

For us the Light has come and His Name is Jesus. As we truly follow Him we will not walk in darkness.

However, in our ministry, we find those who say they are Christians but seem to be walking in darkness rather than light. These people, it seems, at one time prayed for Jesus to save them, but they are not following Him as they should follow Him. They have accepted Christ as their Saviour but have not made Him Lord of their lives.

Many times I hear wives say, "My husband is a Christian (has accepted Christ) but he won't go to church.

He doesn't read the Bible and he prays only when we ask the blessing before meals. He comes home drunk once or twice a week and he is selfish and mean to the children and me," etc.

These men may have their "ticket" to heaven and eternal life, but it is obvious they are not walking in the *"light of life"* and following Jesus as He desires them to. They have not made Him Lord or boss of their lives. Probably all of you know men or women like this. Today I would like our prayer to be for them.

Prayer: "Lord, I lift up _____ to You right now. I come against the rebellion that is in his/her life. I bless him/her with a thirst for righteousness and a desire to walk in Your ways. I come against bitterness and selfishness and say they will be replaced with forgiveness and an unselfish and loving attitude.

"Satan, in Jesus' Name, I command you to loose _____ from bondage to you and I say _____ is now free to choose God's will for him/her.

"In the strong Name of Jesus, Amen."

Today's Scripture Reading: John 8:12-47

Week 26 Day 7
Children of Light

...you are light in the Lord. Live as children of light (for the fruit of the light consists in all goodness, righteousness and truth). Ephesians 5:8, 9

Because of our relationship with God, we are children of light and that position carries a great responsibility.

Our good works are to be bringing glory to our

Father. If you are a parent, you know what a wonderful feeling it is to you when your children are well-behaved and do what you have taught them. It is great to have children who walk in godly ways and bring joy to your heart.

Many parents also know the hurt and sorrow that comes when a child is rebellious and does not follow the godly path they have prayed he would go.

I'm sure God has many of the same feelings about us. I'm sure we bring joy to His heart when we live as children of light walking in righteousness and truth. And I'm sure His heart aches when we do not walk in His ways, causing our light before others to be dimmed and bringing dishonor to the Name of Jesus.

You can be sure the world is watching those of us who call ourselves Christians to see if we are walking in the light we profess.

Prayer: "Dear Heavenly Father, I am Your child. As Your child, please help me to walk in Your pure light. May my light not be dimmed by anything that is contrary to Your righteousness. Help me to walk in the light as He, Jesus, was and is in the Light.
"In His Name, Amen."

Today's Scripture Reading: Matt. 13:24-29, 36-52.
(Note especially verse 43)

Order Form

Please send me _____ copies
of Vol. I of *Image to Image,* at
$5.00 per copy. $_____

Please send me _____ copies
of Vol. II of *Image to Image,* at
$5.00 per copy. $_____

Please send me _____ copies
of *Set My Heart Free,* at $5.00
per copy. $_____

Total Enclosed $_____

You may use: Mastercard
               Visa   _____
               Personal Check   _____
               Money Order   _____

If using your credit card, please give us the following
information.

Credit card #_____
Expiration date_____

(Please do not send cash).

Please tear out this order form and mail along with
check, money order, or credit card information to:

Derin's Coffee Shop
P.O. Box 2042
Windsor, CO 80550